Foundations of Faith:
Education for New Church Members

Teacher's Guide

by Michael D. Bush and Zeta T. Lamberson

edited by Laura B. Lewis,
Richard R. Osmer, and
Amy S. Vaughn

Book design by Carol Johnson

Cover design by Sharon Adams

PRINTED IN THE UNITED STATES OF AMERICA

ISBN 0-664-50094-3

About the Authors

Michael D. Bush is pastor of Westminster Presbyterian Church in Mobile, Alabama. Prior to assuming this pastorate, he served as pastor of Trinity Presbyterian Church in Richmond, Virginia, and as interim pastor of two congregations in New Jersey. He is a graduate of the University of Kentucky, Union Theological Seminary in Virginia, Yale University, and is a Ph.D. candidate at Princeton Theological Seminary. Michael and his wife, Janellyn, are the parents of three children and are lifelong Presbyterians.

Zeta Touchton Lamberson grew up in Columbia, South Carolina. She attended Presbyterian College in Clinton, South Carolina, where she majored in Elementary Education and minored in Christian Education. She went on to receive a Masters in Religious Education from the Presbyterian School of Christian Education in Richmond, Virginia, in 1977. Zeta served churches in Virginia, South Carolina, and West Virginia as a Church Educator for ten years before enrolling in the seminary. She graduated from Columbia Theological Seminary with a MDiv in 1991. Since graduation and ordination, Zeta has served as the Minister of Program Coordination and Education at Peachtree Presbyterian Church in Atlanta, Georgia. While at Peachtree, Zeta edited *Stepping Stones on the Journey to Faith,* a guidebook for children, youth, and adults on the basics of the faith every Christian should know. She and her husband, Bill, have two children, Zeta Elizabeth and Bart.

Contents

Introduction

This eight-session course is designed to teach Christians the foundations of our faith. Based on the Apostles' Creed and the section of the *Study Catechism* that expounds on the Apostles' Creed, this resource provides an opportunity for Christians to consider what the church confesses, our own reflections on this material, and what it means for how we live our lives.

While written expressly as education for new church members, this course is easily adaptable to a number of settings in the life of the church (See "Contexts for Use" on page 2). The purpose of this course is not to prepare participants to pass a test on church history, to memorize Christian doctrine, or to sit through a requisite number of boring lectures before joining the church. Rather, it provides opportunities for participants to reflect upon and discuss what is at stake in joining the church and confessing with the church what we believe. This course is a chance for group members to reflect on the very important decision whether or not to publicly affirm their faith in joining the church. The course explores what is at stake in church membership by teaching the content of the Apostles' Creed, providing tools for critical reflection on this content, and guiding participants to discover the implications for their life.

Imagine your typical class for adults considering church membership. It probably includes lifelong Presbyterians who have moved to your town and are seeking to transfer membership; parents of young children who have not been involved in a church since their own youth but now hope to have their children baptized; members, both lapsed and active, of Catholic and other Protestant churches who are unfamiliar with the Presbyterian Church; and those who were raised outside of any Christian tradition and come seeking baptism as well as church membership. *Foundations of Faith* recognizes and embraces this likely diversity. New Christians and those who have not participated in Christian education since childhood will find the material basic, accessible, and free of intimidating jargon. Veteran church members will find in this course much more than a review session. It represents a unique opportunity for renewal and serious reflection.

Structure of the Course

This course is built around the Apostles' Creed and the *Study Catechism* of the Presbyterian Church (U.S.A.). The Apostles' Creed is the most ancient creed of the Christian Church still in use today. It began with the Roman baptismal creed in the second century A.D. and developed into its present form by the ninth century A.D. It is not a Presbyterian creed, but rather the most widely used confessional statement in the Western church. By focusing on the Apostles' Creed, we affirm that our central identity is that of Christian and that we confess our faith with the church universal.

The *Study Catechism* was approved for use as a teaching tool for the church at the 210th General Assembly in June 1998. It provides commentary in question-and-answer form on the Apostles' Creed, the Ten Commandments, and the Lord's Prayer. The *Study Catechism* provides us with a distinctively Reformed and Presbyterian understanding of the Christian faith. *Foundations of Faith* works with the section of the *Study Catechism* that covers the Apostles' Creed. A companion piece to this resource, *Devotion and Discipline: Training for Presbyterian Leaders*, is based on the Ten Commandments and the Lord's Prayer sections of the *Study Catechism.*

The course is divided into eight sessions designed to last seventy-five to ninety minutes each. In addition to the lesson plans, the *Teacher's Guide* includes theological background material, scripture references, resources for further study, and the catechism questions and answers. The accompanying *Student Guide* provides participants with the catechism questions and answers, scripture references, background material, and guidance and space for journaling.

Contexts for Use

NEW CHURCH MEMBER EDUCATION

This course is designed expressly for the new church member. As a study guide for the Apostles' Creed, it focuses on what is at stake in confessing Christian faith as a member of the church. Offer this course as preparation for those seeking church membership or as follow-up for those who have recently joined the church. Participants in this course will gain not only a solid Reformed understanding of the basic Christian beliefs but the ability to reflect theologically on matters of faith and life.

PREPARATION FOR A SERVICE OF BAPTISMAL RENEWAL

This course represents an excellent opportunity for church members to prepare for a service of baptismal renewal. Consider offering this course in the weeks preceding a planned service of baptismal renewal. If you choose this option, add a discussion of the significance of baptismal renewal and the service of baptismal renewal to the session on the sacraments (session 7).

EDUCATION FOR COLLEGE STUDENTS OR YOUNG ADULTS

This course would be especially appropriate as education for college students (either those home for the summer, or those visiting your church for the school year if you are in a college community). It offers them an opportunity for intelligent, critical reflection on their faith and their continued church membership. *Foundations of Faith* would also work well for young adults who were raised in the church but who have not had an opportunity as adults to study and reflect on their faith.

GENERAL ADULT EDUCATION

While geared toward new members, this course can be easily adapted to fit any adult education program. Many church members do not have a solid grasp of the basics of Christian faith and would welcome an opportunity for significant discussion and reflection upon the Apostles' Creed. Offer this course as a Sunday morning class (you may have to shorten the sessions somewhat to fit the standard one-hour slot), a Lenten midweek study, or a special summer class. The material could also be adapted for use on a weekend retreat. Cover sessions 1–5 on the retreat and then offer sessions 6–8 as follow-up classes after you return.

How to Use This Resource

What You Will Need

Every class member will need a copy of *Foundations of Faith Student Guide*. This booklet contains the relevant *Study Catechism* questions and answers, background information, and space for keeping a journal. If possible, distribute the student guides in advance so that class members can prepare for the first group session. In addition to the *Student Guide*, please make sure that every class member has a Bible available at the group sessions. A section in each lesson plan outlines materials you will need for teaching. You will need newsprint or a wipe board and markers for every class session.

Preparation Prior to Group Sessions

- Be familiar with all of the components of the lesson plan. Read through all of the background material and supporting scripture passages before class, jotting down any notes or comments in the margins.

- Where options are given, decide whether you will divide your class into smaller groups or stay together.

- Prepare any handouts or information to be posted at the front of the room.

- Mark in the margins the times you expect to start and complete each item in the lesson plan (e.g., Opening Activity 7:45–8:00 P.M.). This will help you to keep the discussion flowing and let you know easily whether you are running ahead of schedule or behind.

- The lesson plans are designed for a seventy-five- to ninety-minute class. If you have less time available, be sure to go over the plan carefully to decide which portions you will omit.

For Every Session You Will Find

THE *STUDY CATECHISM*

Each session begins with the relevant questions and answers from the *Study Catechism* along with the supporting scripture references.

THEOLOGICAL BACKGROUND

This background material serves as a brief commentary on the catechism. Read this section as you prepare to lead the group session.

FOR FURTHER STUDY

This brief section suggests books that pursue covered topics in greater depth.

PREPARATION AND MATERIALS NEEDED

This section summarizes what you need to do to prepare to lead the group session and lists the materials you will need.

THE LESSON PLAN

Welcome and Review

Each session begins with a brief recap of the previous lessons. This exercise is intended to help participants form a "big picture" view of the Apostles' Creed and to reinforce connections between the sections.

Getting Started

This section of the lesson includes an opening activity to introduce the topic and get people talking as well as introductory remarks. You may either read the introductory remarks or put the content into your own words.

What Does the Church Confess?

When we confess our faith we say what we believe publicly and in so doing we commit our lives to it. This section of the discussion examines what it is that the church confesses in the Apostles' Creed. The *Study Catechism* is used as a tool for understanding how the Presbyterian Church has interpreted the creed.

What Do I Think?

The Presbyterian Church has always placed a high priority on having a reflective faith. It is important for the church and for individual believers to reflect upon what it is we believe and to engage in a critical appropriation of those beliefs rather than a mindless and passive repetition of words we have been taught. This section of the discussion seeks to help class members construct and articulate their theological understanding of the faith we confess. It provides opportunities to think, raise questions, struggle with implications, and make affirmations. Here, the *Study Catechism* works as guide and conversation partner. The catechism serves as a springboard for serious reflection, criticism, and dialogue. Remember, it is important to encourage the participants to enter into a dialogue with the catechism, criticizing it when they do not agree and allowing themselves to be questioned by it as well. In short, encourage open and free reflection during this period.

What Does This Mean for Me Today?

Sometimes we think of the Apostles' Creed as simply a bunch of tired old words that we repeat mindlessly in worship. Confessing the Apostles' Creed is a nice tradition; it is one of those things we do. The reality is that confessing this creed will change the way we live. When we join as members of Christ's church and together confess the Apostles' Creed, we commit our lives to the faith we profess. Christian faith is not just an assent to certain truths, it is a way of life. This section of the discussion explores connections between what we believe and who we are and how we live our lives. We will look at questions such as "What is our purpose in life?" "How are we supposed to get along with difficult neighbors?" and "How should I treat people of other faiths?"

Closing

Each session ends with suggestions for closing your time together with prayer or an affirmation of faith.

The *Foundations of Faith Student Guide*

The *Student Guide* is an integral part of this course. Participants will have ready access to the catechism questions and scripture references during class. The background material and suggestions for journaling are intended as preparation for the group session. If possible, distribute the student guides prior to the first group session so that class members can prepare for the first session. The preparation offered in the *Student Guide* will greatly enrich the discussions in the group sessions. In addition, the suggestions for journaling, scripture reading, and prayer are intended to help participants form or strengthen habits of personal spiritual disciplines.

Each session of the *Student Guide* includes suggestions for keeping a journal and blank space in which to write. There are usually two options for the journal each week. The first suggestion involves reading through the catechism questions a second time and choosing a sentence or phrase to reflect on throughout the week. The second is a suggestion based on the content of the session. Ideally, participants will be able to set some time aside for the journal each day and will be able to use both suggestions each week in addition to reading the background material. It is fine, however, for participants to choose only one activity on which to focus.

Here are some ways for you to help make using the *Student Guide* a success for your group.

1. Make sure that you have a copy of the *Student Guide.*

2. Read through the introduction to the *Student Guide.*

3. Read through the instructions for keeping a journal in the Introduction of the *Student Guide.* The process of choosing a phrase from the catechism to reflect on throughout the week has its roots in Christian contemplative practices. Our hope is that through this practice, participants will become accustomed to bringing scripture and affirmations of faith into conversation with their daily lives.

4. Keep a journal yourself.

5. Ask class members how the journal is going at each group session. Provide an opportunity after opening prayer for them to share their reflections from the journal.

6. Encourage class members to give this exercise a serious and thoughtful try. Acknowledge that it is often difficult to form new habits but that the benefit can far outweigh the inconvenience.

What Is God's Purpose for My Life?

The *Study Catechism:* Questions 1–5

Question 1. What is God's purpose for your life?

God wills that I should live by the grace of the Lord Jesus Christ, for the love of God, and in the communion of the Holy Spirit.

2 Cor. 13:13

Question 2. How do you live by the grace of the Lord Jesus Christ?

I am not my own. I have been bought with a price. The Lord Jesus Christ loved me and gave himself for me. I entrust myself completely to his care, giving thanks each day for his wonderful goodness.

1 Cor. 6:19–20   Ps. 136:1

Gal. 2:20

Question 3. How do you live for the love of God?

I love because God first loved me. God loves me in Christ with a love that never ends. Amazed by grace, I no longer live for myself. I live for the Lord who died and rose again, triumphant over death, for my sake. Therefore, I take those around me to heart, especially those in particular need, knowing that Christ died for them no less than for me.

1 John 4:19   Rom. 12:15–16

2 Cor. 5:15

Question 4. How do you live in the communion of the Holy Spirit?

By the Holy Spirit, I am made one with the Lord Jesus Christ. I am baptized into Christ's body, the church, along with all others who confess him by faith. As a member of this community, I trust in God's Word, share in the Lord's Supper, and turn to God constantly in prayer. As I grow in grace and knowledge, I am led to do the good works that God intends for my life.

1 Cor. 12:27   1 Cor. 6:17, 19

Gal. 3:27   Eph. 2:10

2 Pet. 3:18

Question 5. What does a Christian believe?

All that is promised in the gospel. A summary is found in the Apostles' Creed, which affirms the main content of the Christian faith.

John 20:31

Theological Background

The *Study Catechism* in its first question recalls the beloved first question of the Westminster Shorter Catechism, which was the backbone of Christian education in the Presbyterian Church for three hundred years. That seventeenth-century catechism began, "What is the chief end of man? To glorify God and enjoy Him forever."

Like the Shorter Catechism, the *Study Catechism* begins by placing human life within the larger context of God's purpose for the world. Behind the question, *What is God's purpose for your life?* lies the conviction that life is meaningful and has purpose. We exist for a reason. Life and history are moving toward an end and a fulfillment that God has in mind. Time is a line that begins and ends in heaven, in the presence of God; it is not a circle that goes round and round hopelessly and forever. Every person and event is unique and unrepeatable, and therefore everything is significant. Although from our perspective many unforeseen, ironic, and even tragic circumstances can bring a person into existence, no one is a mistake from the perspective of heaven. Every human life, and all of human life, has purpose.

The *Study Catechism* explains the purposefulness of life by paraphrasing words of the Apostle Paul, found in the Bible at 2 Corinthians

13:13, words that are commonly known as the "apostolic benediction," and are often part of the blessing or benediction at the conclusion of our worship services. In the catechism's use of this verse, there is power in the prepositions it adds: *by* the grace of our Lord Jesus Christ; *for* the love of God; *in* the communion of the Holy Spirit. To live "by the grace of our Lord Jesus Christ" means to live with the grace we have received in Jesus Christ as our standard. The popular question, *What would Jesus do*? leads us along this line, but in the end turns out to be too simple. What Jesus would do in a given situation, being God living a human life, is not an infallible guide, because what Jesus would do is not necessarily the same thing he expects me to do as I live by the grace with which he has treated me. According to Scripture (for example, Luke 6:8), Jesus was able to exercise God's all-knowing power to see people and situations as God sees them. We cannot do that, and so must treat people, as John Calvin put it, "exercising a judgment of charity"; a judgment, that is, of grace. That does not mean we become ethical doormats, condoning whatever anyone feels is right. It does, however, mean that we think of what God has forgiven in us before we draw hard and fast conclusions about others. To live by the grace of our Lord Jesus Christ is to ask, *What does Jesus Christ expect me to do if I am to reflect the power of his grace in my life?*

To live "for the love of God" means to live in a way that advances in the world the cause of God's love, as expressed normatively and finally in Jesus Christ. The alternative, as the *Study Catechism* recognizes, is to live "for myself." Being freed in Jesus Christ from the need to be my own top-priority project, I am able to invest myself in the lives of others, especially those who are poor in spirit or in the necessities of life.

To live "in the communion of the Holy Spirit" means first of all, as the catechism points out, to live within the life of the church, the Body of Christ. Only in the second place does it involve doing good works. When this order is reversed, we produce an individualistic Christianity that has little in common with the biblical vision of the church. The communion of the Holy Spirit does, however, have a personal aspect. Every Christian lives in fellowship with the Holy Spirit in the sense that our faith is the reality of the Holy Spirit within us. John Calvin and many Reformed thinkers after him held that faith is less our achievement and decision than it is the genuine and real presence of the Spirit of God in our lives.

Jonathan Edwards described the kind of dedicated Christian life the catechism envisions as "living to God." In other words, the Christian life is oriented to God as both its source and its goal.

For Further Study

For historical perspective, John H. Leith and Ronald Wallace have both written on John Calvin's doctrine of the Christian life. See Leith, *John Calvin's Doctrine of the Christian Life* (Louisville, Ky.: Westminster/John Knox Press, 1989); and Wallace, *Calvin's Doctrine of the Christian Life* (Eugene, Ore.: Wipf and Stock, Publishers, 1997).

Preparation and Materials Needed

- Read over carefully the background material and the lesson plan.
- Make decisions where necessary about optional activities, whether to divide into small groups, etc.
- Prepare a large copy of the "Top Ten Fears about Participating in a Class for New Church Members" (page 19). Blow it up on your copy machine so that it is as large as possible.
- Write the instructions for small groups (page 15) on a sheet of newsprint.
- Provide nametags and markers.
- Provide markers or color-coded label stickers for the "Top Ten Fears" activity.
- Have newsprint or a wipe board available.

Lesson Plan—Session 1: What Is God's Purpose for Our Life? Questions 1–5

As Class Members Arrive

- Have nametags available for participants to fill out.
- Post the large copy of the "Top Ten Fears about Participating in a Class for New Church Members" (page 19) at the front of the room. As participants arrive, give them a colored marker or a small round sticker (color-coded labels work well) and ask each person to place a mark or a sticker by the "fear" he or she most closely feels. Reassure them that this is an icebreaker activity and that you are not looking for a correct answer.

Introductions

Welcome the group and invite them to introduce themselves. Ask each person to share the following:

- their name
- something significant about themselves (work, family, etc.)
- their experience with church as a child (Recognize that some people grew up in this denomination and they perhaps are familiar with aspects of church life, while others maybe were raised outside of the church. Acknowledge up front that you are not assuming that everyone grew up in the church.)

GETTING STARTED: INTRODUCE THE COURSE

Draw the group's attention to the "Top Ten Fears" poster at the front of the room and note the two or three fears with the most marks on them. Tell the group that you expect this course to allay those fears and that you hope they have some positive expectations for the experience as well.

Invite the class to break into groups of three or four and to share some of their positive expectations for the course. **What do you hope to learn or accomplish over the next eight sessions?**

After you bring the class back together, ask for three or four volunteers to share with the whole group something they mentioned.

Introductory Remarks

(Read or summarize the following material for the class.)

Purpose of the Course

The purpose of this course is not to prepare you to pass a test or to memorize a bunch of dogma or to provide a hoop you have to jump through before joining the church. Rather, it is an opportunity for you to reflect upon and discuss what is at stake in joining the church and confessing with the church what we believe. Joining the church is a significant and life-changing decision. Sometimes it seems as though affiliating with a church is much like joining any other positive social organization. In reality, it is completely different from joining the Rotary or the Junior League or a sorority or fraternity. This course provides a chance for you to reflect on your very important decision whether or not to affirm your faith publicly in joining the church.

Some of you may be thinking, "I've been a church member for years and I'm just switching towns (or denominations, or congregations). I can say the Apostles' Creed by heart and I understand what it means to be a church member." For you, this course is not going to be a review session, but rather an opportunity for renewal and reflection. This study will remind you as well of what is at stake in aligning yourself with Christ's Church and confessing the creed.

The focus of our time together will be on the foundations of our faith—the basic building blocks of what we as Christians believe. We will study the Apostles' Creed together and in so doing we will not only cover what the creed says, but also our own reflections on its content and its implications for our daily life.

Structure of the Course

This course is built around the Apostles' Creed and the *Study Catechism* of the Presbyterian Church (U.S.A.). The Apostles' Creed is the most ancient creed of the Christian Church still in use today. It began with the Roman baptismal creed in the second century A.D. and developed into its present form by the ninth century A.D. It is not a Presbyterian creed, but rather the most widely used confessional statement in the Western church. By focusing on the Apostles' Creed, we affirm that our central identity is that of Christian and that we confess our faith with the church universal.

The *Study Catechism* was approved for use as a teaching tool for the church at the 210th General Assembly in June 1998. It provides commentary in question-and-answer form on the Apostles' Creed, the Ten Commandments, and the Lord's Prayer. The *Study Catechism* provides us with a distinctively Reformed and Presbyterian understanding of the Christian faith. It gives us a Reformed angle on a creed that we share in common with both Catholic and Protestant churches.

Our discussion each week will include three sections.

1. What Does the Church Confess?

   The Presbyterian Church is a confessional church. That is to say, we hold onto certain creeds and confessions (found in the *Book of Confessions*) that state what we believe. These statements are an effort to say to ourselves, our neighbors, and the rest of the world who we are and what we believe. When we confess our faith we say what we believe publicly and in so doing we commit our lives to it. In this section of our discussion each week, we will examine what it is that the church confesses in the Apostles' Creed. We will use the *Study Catechism* as a tool for understanding how the Presbyterian Church has interpreted the creed.

2. What Do I Think?

   The Presbyterian Church had always placed a high priority on having a reflective faith. It is important for the church and for individual believers to reflect upon what it is we believe and to engage in a critical appropriation of those beliefs rather than a mindless and passive repetition of words we have been taught. In this section of our discussion we will be cultivating a reflective faith. We will have opportunities to think, raise questions, struggle with implications, and make affirmations. Here, the *Study Catechism* becomes our guide and conversation partner. The catechism serves as a springboard for serious reflection, criticism, and dialogue. Through our discussion, we hope you will be better able to construct and articulate your theological understanding of the faith we confess.

3. What Does This Mean for Me Today?

Sometimes we think of the Apostles' Creed as simply a bunch of tired old words that we repeat mindlessly in worship. Confessing the Apostles' Creed is a nice tradition, one of those things we do. The reality is that confessing this creed will change the way we live. When we join as members of Christ's church and together confess the Apostles' Creed, we commit our lives to the faith we profess. Christian faith is not just an assent to certain truths, it is a way of life. In this section of our discussion we will explore connections between what we believe and who we are and how we live our lives. We will look at questions like, "What is our purpose in life? How are we supposed to get along with difficult neighbors?" and "How should I treat people of other faiths?" Here is where we figure out what is at stake in our decision to profess publicly Jesus Christ as Lord and Savior.

Let's begin. . . .

WHAT DOES THE CHURCH CONFESS?

1. Read *Study Catechism* questions 1–5 responsively. Have one person read the questions and the rest of the group respond with the answers. Direct class members to page 4 in the *Student Guide* to find the appropriate section of the catechism.

2. Ask class members to turn to 2 Corinthians 13:13 in their Bibles and invite a volunteer to read it aloud. Ask, **2 Corinthians is a letter from Paul to the Church in Corinth. Where in the letter is this verse found? What function does it play in the letter? Can anyone recall what is the last thing the pastor does in the worship service just before the postlude?**

3. Tell the group: the *Study Catechism* begins with a benediction. Usually we find benedictions at the end: either at the end of a letter or the end of a worship service. Here the catechism picks up where we leave off in worship. As Christians, the rhythm of our week is

formed by corporate worship and then going out into the world to live as followers of Christ. The catechism begins with the benediction that sends us out and gives purpose to our daily lives.

4. Forced Choice Exercise

    Give class members a moment to look over the catechism's answer to the question "What is God's purpose for my life?" (questions 2, 3, and 4). Ask them each to choose which is their initial favorite of those questions and answers, perhaps the one they feel is most interesting or the one that speaks to them most clearly. Designate three corners of the room as questions 2, 3, and 4 and ask class members to go the corner of the room that represents the question they chose.

    Ask the groups that form to do the following: (You might want to write these instructions on a sheet of newsprint before class and post it on the wall at this time).

    Look up the scripture passages that are listed as references for your question. (References are found in the *Student Guide*.) Answer the following questions:

    - Discuss the portions of the answers that come from the scripture. How does the catechism answer, expand on, or explain the scripture passage?
    - In your question, what is God's first action (or actions) toward us?
    - What does the catechism offer as our appropriate response to that action?
    - How does God's action enable or empower that response?

    Invite the groups to come back together. Ask one person from each group to share their group's answer to "What is God's first action toward us?" and "What does the catechism offer as our appropriate response to that action?"

    Look now to question 5. **What answer does it give to the question, "What does a Christian believe?"**

    The prologue of the catechism gives us a concise summary of the gospel: what God has done for us. By beginning with grace, love, and communion, the catechism sets out how our confession of faith (the Apostles' Creed) is a response to the gospel. We begin with the assurance that we are firmly held in the grace of our Lord Jesus Christ, the love of God, and the communion of the Holy Spirit. This trilogy not only helps us to understand God's purpose for our lives, but provides a framework and a foundation for what is to come as we explore the Apostles' Creed.

What Do I Think?

If your group is larger than twelve, you might consider breaking up into smaller groups of five or six for this portion of the discussion. Choose several of the following issues to discuss. Remember, it is important to encourage the participants to enter into a dialogue with the catechism, criticizing it when they do not agree and allowing themselves to be questioned by it as well. In short, encourage open and free reflection during this period.

1. Invite the group to share any questions or comments they have about the questions and answers. Is there a phrase you particularly like? Is there a sentence or concept that is unclear or that you disagree with? If you could choose one phrase to hang on to, what would it be and why?

2. What does it mean to have been bought with a price? Is your initial reaction to this positive or negative? What comfort does it give to know you belong to God? What fears, anxieties, or rebellions does it prompt?

3. What are some ways that we as humans tend to live for ourselves? What does it look like to live for the Lord?

4. Many people of wide-ranging religious beliefs engage in significant service to others. Does it make a difference to believe that our service is motivated out of God's initial love for us, that we take those around us to heart not out of an abstract sense of altruism, but because we believe that Christ died for them no less than for us?

5. What are some of the blessings of being a part of the Christian community, i.e., the church? What distinguishes the communion of the Holy Spirit from simple community or a gathering of friends?

6. Turn to a neighbor and reflect on a time when you were "led to do a good work." What were the circumstances? How did you experience God's leading in your life? When you bring the group back together, ask for three or four volunteers to share briefly ways that they experienced God's leading in their lives.

7. Imagine that you have an adolescent son or daughter—around seventeen or eighteen—who is trying to decide where or whether to go to college and is in the midst of a frustrating struggle to understand his or her purpose in life. All those big teenage questions are

surfacing: "What's the point, anyway? What am I supposed to do with my life? Who is going to love me? Why should I bother?" How would you weave affirmations from the prologue of the *Study Catechism* or the accompanying scripture references into a discussion of life's purpose with him or her? (If it is too much of a stretch to imagine having such a conversation with your own son or daughter, imagine instead a Christian friend who is going through a midlife crisis.)

WHAT DOES THIS MEAN FOR ME TODAY?

1. **What are some of the things that give life meaning and purpose? What initially comes to your mind?**

   Write responses on newsprint or a wipe board.

2. Let's look now at the catechism question and response. **How can this serve as a framework for our life's meaning and purpose?**

   Review God's actions and our responses from questions 2–4.

God's Action	Our Response
Grace	Trust
Love	Love for God and others
Communion	Growth—Becoming who I was created to be

   God's action and our response give our life meaning and frame the way we live. Our confession of faith is connected to purpose and to how we understand and live out our lives.

3. **Which is more difficult for you: to entrust yourself completely to God's care, to take those around you to heart—especially those in particular need—or to "turn to God constantly in prayer"?** Answer this question privately in your journal.

4. Bring the group back together. Ask the group to list roadblocks to each of these actions—entrusting yourself completely to God's care, taking those around you to heart, turning to God constantly in prayer—and write the responses on newsprint or the board.

   Then list affirmations, what enables us, and what compels us to trust, to love, and to commune with God in prayer. Suggest that they use material from the catechism questions (e.g., "because God first loved me"), from the accompanying scripture verses (e.g., God is good; God's steadfast love endures forever), or from personal experience (e.g., I have a difficult time praying on my own, but the prayers in worship are very meaningful to me and help me learn to pray to God).

5. Ask group members to think of a decision facing them in the week or month ahead. It could be a major decision (such as whether or not to change jobs or move your elderly parent to a nursing home) or a smaller decision (such as an issue at work, what tactic to take in getting your six-year-old to eat his dinner, or what to do on Friday night). Pick a phrase from the catechism and think about how it might influence your decision. Turn to a neighbor and share your pending decision and your thoughts on it. (If the decision facing you is confidential, you may choose to speak of it in general terms.)

CLOSING

1. Introduce the *Foundations of Faith Student Guide* if you have not done so already. Encourage group members to use the *Student Guides* to prepare for their next session together. (They should skip to session 2 after reading the introductory material if they did not receive and use their *Student Guides* in advance of this first class.)

2. Close with prayer.

Top Ten Fears about Participating in a Course for New Church Members

1. I will have to pass a test at the end.

2. Other people will realize that I don't know anything about the Bible.

3. It will be boring.

4. I'll have to memorize a bunch of facts about Presbyterians.

5. I'm a new Christian, so the concepts will be over my head.

6. I've been a church member for years in another town, so this will be a superficial review of what I've been taught all my life.

7. It will bring back bad memories of confirmation class when I was thirteen.

8. Someone will ask me why I haven't been to church since I was confirmed.

9. The pastor will learn my name and then will notice if I am not in worship every Sunday.

10. The content will be totally irrelevant to the rest of my life.

Who Is God?

The *Study Catechism*: Questions 6–14

Question 6. What is the first article of the Apostles' Creed?

"I believe in God the Father Almighty, Maker of heaven and earth."

Question 7. What do you believe when you confess your faith in "God the Father Almighty"?

That God is a God of love, and that God's love is powerful beyond measure.

    Lam. 3:22   1 John 4:8

    Song 8:7

Question 8. How do you understand the love and power of God?

Through Jesus Christ. In his life of compassion, his death on the cross, and his resurrection from the dead, I see how vast is God's love for the world—a love that is ready to suffer for our sakes, yet so strong that nothing will prevail against it.

    John 3:16   Matt. 9:36

    Heb. 1:3   1 John 4:9

    Ps. 106:8

Question 9. What comfort do you receive from this truth?

This powerful and loving God is the one whose promises I may trust in all the circumstances of my life, and to whom I belong in life and in death.

Ps. 12:6   Rom. 8:38–39

Question 10. Do you make this confession only as an individual?

No. With the apostles, prophets and martyrs, with all those through the ages who have loved the Lord Jesus Christ, and with all who strive to serve him on earth here and now, I confess my faith in the God of loving power and powerful love.

Heb. 12:1   Rom. 1:12

Question 11. When the creed speaks of "God the Father," does it mean that God is male?

No. Only creatures having bodies can be either male or female. But God has no body, since by nature God is Spirit. Holy Scripture reveals God as a living God beyond all sexual distinctions. Scripture uses diverse images for God, female as well as male. We read, for example, that God will no more forget us than a woman can forget her nursing child (Isa. 49:15). "As a mother comforts her child, so will I comfort you," says the Lord (Isa. 66:13).

Is. 49:15   Matt. 23:37

Is. 66:13

Question 12. Why then does the creed speak of God the Father?

First, because God is identified in the New Testament as the Father of our Lord Jesus Christ. Second, because Jesus Christ is the eternal Son of this Father. Third, because when we are joined to Christ through faith, we are adopted as sons and daughters into the relationship he enjoys with his Father.

Rom. 1:7

John 14:9–10   John 17:24

John 1:12   Gal. 4:6

Question 13. When you confess the God and Father of our Lord Jesus Christ, are you elevating men over women and endorsing male domination?

No. Human power and authority are trustworthy only as they reflect God's mercy and kindness, not abusive patterns of domination. As Jesus taught his disciples, "The greatest among you will be your servant" (Matt. 23:11). God the Father sets the standard by which all misuses of power are exposed and condemned. "Call no one your father on earth," said Jesus, "for you have one Father—the one in heaven" (Matt. 23:9). In fact God calls women and men to all ministries of the church.

Gal. 3:28   Eph. 5:21

Question 14. If God's love is powerful beyond measure, why is there so much evil in the world?

No one can say why, for evil is a terrible abyss beyond all rational explanation. Its ultimate origin is obscure. Its enormity perplexes us. Nevertheless, we boldly affirm that God's triumph over evil is certain. In Jesus Christ God suffers with us, knowing all our sorrows. In raising him from the dead, God gives new hope to the world. Our Lord Jesus Christ, crucified and risen, is himself God's promise that suffering will come to an end, that death shall be no more, and that all things will be made new.

Ps. 23:4   Rom. 8:21

1 Pet. 1:3   Job 19:25

2 Pet. 3:13

Theological Background

The *Study Catechism* calls the Apostles' Creed a summary of the "main content of the Christian faith" (question 5). In so saying, the catechism makes the ancient, important, and today strikingly countercultural affirmation that the faith by which we live is not mere sentiment or a disposition of our lives, but is something that may be to a great extent spoken of and evaluated rationally and imaginatively.

Christian belief is more than feeling or experience. It is a life formed around definite and intelligible truths. "It is noteworthy," writes Karl Barth, "that, apart from this first expression 'I believe,' [the Apostles' Creed] is silent upon the subjective fact of faith. . . . What interests me is not myself with my faith, but He in whom I believe."[1] This is the approach the *Study Catechism* takes as well: It passes silently by the fact of faith as a reality of human history and psychology, and focuses upon the God in whom we believe.

THE GOD OF LOVE

The Apostles' Creed opens with an affirmation of faith in "God the Father Almighty." This is a highly appropriate opening for the Creed, but has to be interpreted with care. Our faith is at root faith in God. As Karl Barth points out, our faith rests first of all in the one God, rather than in any particular "person" of the Trinity. The God in whom we confess our faith is the God of self-giving love. This insight must inform whatever we say about God. It does not mean that God is a God of warm feelings, but of quite concrete compassion. Our knowledge of God comes to us in the biblical witness to Christ's compassionate life, his death by crucifixion, and his resurrection from the dead, which clearly demonstrate the vastness of God's love for the world. As Arthur C. McGill has written, "Christian faith looks upon Jesus as the power of the one and only God from whom all other powers in heaven and earth derive their real powerfulness. If Jesus discloses the unopposable power of love, it can only be because this love is the power of God . . . "[2]

GOD THE FATHER

The affirmation that God may be addressed and affirmed as Father (questions 6–13) has become problematic for many today. Some theologians, along with those who have had alienated or abusive relationships with their fathers, have quite understandably raised the question whether affirming the fatherhood of God does not imply an endorsement of the alienation and abuse in their experience. The *Study Catechism* powerfully affirms this as a valid concern, while still affirming that our confession of God's fatherhood is not disposable. Instead, we believe God the Father judges and rejects the sin that has caused this pain.

The fatherhood of God has its basic context in the doctrine of the Trinity, in the sense that the first person of the Trinity is the Father of the Son, who lived a human life in Jesus of Nazareth. In this context it is clear that the concept of God as Father is at its heart a relational term, not an abstract analogy or metaphor based on human relationships. Rather, human fathers are fathers only metaphorically and imperfectly speaking. God the Father is the real thing, without the weaknesses and failures that sin creates in human life. Jesus helped us understand this in saying, "Call no one your father on earth, for you have one Father —the one in heaven" (Matt. 23:9).

When his disciples asked him to teach them to pray, Jesus said, "When you pray, say: Father, hallowed be your name" (Luke 11:1–2). In so saying, Jesus invites us also to relate to God as our gracious and caring Father. In another place, the *Study Catechism* speaks of our adoption into God's household where Jesus is personally and originally God's Son. Thus, we as Christ's brothers and sisters are by adoption the children of his Father.

As the catechism points out, this does not mean that God is male, that men are to be elevated over women, or that male domination in church, society, or relationships is God's will. While honoring the other ways scriptures speaks to and of God, the catechism recognizes that the fatherhood of God is not a disposable image of God, but is just as necessary for apprehending God's reality as are these other biblical acknowledgements that maleness is not divine.

THE POWER OF GOD

Almightiness is the only one of the attributes or "perfections" of God that is mentioned in the Apostles' Creed. The *Study Catechism* interprets this attribute of God as speaking of God's genuine and loving power, and so understands God's power in light of God's powerful love. At the root of this attribute of God lies the affirmation that God is "ruler of all," *Pantokrator*, in Greek. Understanding the almightiness of God as God's rule over all means recognizing that nothing God wills for the universe as it exists can finally be impossible. The almightiness of God means there is no gap between God's will and God's power. God is able to do whatever God wills. It has long been tempting for some people to try to contrive verbal conundrums to name things that God could not do, such as making a four-sided triangle, or a table with only one surface. These conundrums have nothing to do with God's loving power but are mere verbal nonsense, a game with words. God's almightiness was never believed to affirm that God could do *anything*, regardless of whether it made logical sense or was in character for God. A stock example is the affirmation that God could not decide any longer to be God. The point of affirming God's almightiness is that God's goodness, power, and will are one.

THE PROBLEM OF EVIL

Thus, however helpful it may be to us to have another serious-minded person think through the problem of evil with us, Rabbi Harold Kushner's famous answer to that problem can never be a satisfactory Christian answer since it assumes God's power can be separated from God's goodness and will. In *When Bad Things Happen to Good People*, Kushner argues that the almightiness, goodness, and all-knowingness of God cannot all be true, and one of them must be denied. He chooses to deny God's almightiness: God knows about our pain, being omniscient, and hurts with us, being good, but cannot do anything about it. The mighty act of God in Jesus Christ, though, shows that God is far from helpless in the face of evil. The suffering and death of Jesus Christ means God knows the power of evil personally. The resurrection of Jesus Christ from death, and in it his defeat of the power of death over life, is God's answer to the problem of evil.

For Further Study

On the history and teaching of the Apostles' Creed, as well as of the Nicene Creed, the definitive resource is still J. N. D. Kelly, *Early Christian Creeds* (New York: Longman, 1972).

For an alternative to Kushner's answer to the problem of evil that is consistent with Christian faith and with the theology of the *Study Catechism*, see especially Austin Farrer, *Love Almighty and Ills Unlimited* (Garden City, N.Y.: Doubleday, 1961). See also C. S. Lewis, *The Problem of Pain* (New York: Macmillan, 1962). Lewis's book was inspired by a desire to answer what he saw as inadequacies in his friend Farrer's book. Of the two, Farrer's work remains the more highly regarded by scholars. An untechnical book, and one far superior to Kushner's for parents who are dealing with the death of a child, is Nicholas Wolterstorff's *Lament for a Son* (Grand Rapids: Wm. B. Eerdmans Publishing Co., 1987).

Preparation and Materials Needed

- Read over carefully the background material and the lesson plan.
- Make decisions where necessary about optional activities, whether to divide into small groups, etc.
- Provide nametags and markers.
- Make copies of the worksheet, "The Apostles' Creed in Question-and-Answer Form" (page 32).
- Write the outline of the first section of the Apostles' Creed (page 27) and the instructions for small group (page 28) on newsprint.
- Have newsprint or a wipe board available.

Lesson Plan—Session 2: Who Is God: Questions 6–14

WELCOME AND REVIEW

Welcome the group and have nametags available to fill out. Invite participants to introduce themselves. Ask each person to share the following information:

- their name
- something they recall about last week's introduction to this course (a new idea or insight, a question, a phrase or image from the *Study Catechism*)
- when and where they first heard or were taught the Apostles' Creed or another creedal statement (Recognize that some may be quite familiar with the Apostles' Creed and others may have had little or no exposure to this or other creeds. Acknowledge up front that you are not assuming that everyone grew up in the church.)

Review Lesson 1 by reading *Study Catechism* questions 1 and 5 responsively from the student journals with one person reading the questions and the group responding.

Question 1. What is God's purpose for your life?

God wills that I should live by the grace of the Lord Jesus Christ, for the love of God, and in the communion of the Holy Spirit.

Question 5. What does a Christian believe?

All that is promised in the gospel. A summary is found in the Apostles' Creed, which affirms the main content of the Christian faith.

Review of the Apostles' Creed

(Follow up the introduction to the Apostles' Creed given in the first session by reading or summarizing the following material for the class.)

The Apostles' Creed is the oldest Christian creedal statement in the Western church. In many churches the congregation says the Apostles' Creed each week in worship. Together they proclaim what Christians believe. This creed also is frequently used when Christians are baptized or profess their faith and join the church. In some congregations the Apostles' Creed is proclaimed in question-and-answer format. Three questions are asked and the congregation responds to each question by saying a portion of the creed.

GETTING STARTED

1. Make copies of the worksheet "The Apostles' Creed in Question-and-Answer Form" (page 32) and distribute them to the class. Invite

the participants to stand and say the Apostles' Creed aloud together in a question-and-answer form. Ask for a volunteer to ask the questions, to which the class will respond by reading each section of the Apostles' Creed in unison.

2. Ask, **What difference, if any, does it make to you to say the Apostles' Creed this way? How did it feel to respond to questions of what you believe? What other differences did you notice?**

3. Invite participants to examine the structure of the Apostles' Creed. Ask, **What are the main sections of the Apostles' Creed?** (It is divided into three main sections or articles.)

4. Ask, **What do these sections tell us about who God is?** The Apostles' Creed is a Trinitarian statement of faith. By means of this creed, Christians confess their faith in the three "persons" of the Trinity: God, Jesus Christ, and the Holy Spirit.

Remind them of the three basic steps that will be followed in the session: What does the church confess? What do I think? What does this mean for me?

WHAT DOES THE CHURCH CONFESS?

1. Provide participants with an overview of the first section of the Apostles' Creed as it is discussed in the *Study Catechism*. (Consider making copies of the following outline or writing the outline on newsprint or wipe board for the class to see.) Point out that the first article deals with God first as "Father Almighty" and second as "Maker of Heaven and Earth." In this lesson we focus on questions 6–14 in the *Study Catechism*.

The First Article of the Apostles' Creed	Question 6
I believe in God the Father Almighty	7
God's Love and Power	8–10
Meaning of "God the Father"	11–13
God's Powerful Love vs. Evil	14
Maker of Heaven and Earth	15
Created in God's Image	16–21
God's Providence and Care	22–24
Creation as God's Act of Grace	25–26
Creation and Modern Science	27

2. Read the *Study Catechism* questions 6–10 responsively. Have one person read the questions and the rest of the group respond with the answers. Direct class members to page 10 in the *Student Guide.*

3. God's Love and God's Power

   The *Study Catechism* interprets the meaning of what we confess when we say "I believe in God, the Father Almighty" in terms of God's love and the power that flows from God's love. Catechism questions 7–9 discuss how we may understand and draw comfort from the powerful love of God as well as God's loving power.

   Divide into groups of three to six people. Ask each group to discuss the following (you may want to write these instructions on a poster or sheet of newsprint):

   - Look up these scripture references for catechism questions 7–9.

     Question 7: Lamentations 3:22, 1 John 4:7–8

     Question 8: John 3:16–7, Hebrews 1:1–3

     Question 9: Psalm 18:30, Romans 8:38–39

   - In each group, discuss the scripture references and what the catechism answers add or explain.

   - For each catechism answer, ask:

     How is God's power and love described here?

     Where do we see God's love and power in action?

     How do God's love and power differ from human understandings of love and power?

   Invite the groups to come back together. Ask one person from each group to share their group's answers to the questions. List questions and responses on wipe board or newsprint.

4. Confessing Our Faith

   Read question 10 responsively. Ask, **What answer does it give to the question, "Do you make this confession only as an individual?"**

   Point out that the Apostles' Creed is written in the first person. When we repeat the words of the Apostles' Creed, we say *I believe.* Also note that although we confess our faith in first person, we do not confess our faith as solitary individuals. We confess our faith "surrounded by a great cloud of witnesses" (Heb. 12:1). Ask, **Why is it important that we make our confession of faith personally by saying "I"?**

Ask, **Why is it also important that we make this confession together with others and not by ourselves?**

5. Speaking of "God the Father"

Invite the class to read catechism questions and answers 11–13 responsively.

These questions raise some contemporary concerns with respect to human beings—both females and males—and how we understand the nature of God. For this exercise you may choose to divide into three or more groups or work together on each *Catechism* question. (If you choose to work in groups, be sure that each group shares its findings with the whole class.)

- Group 1: Is God Male?

  Look at catechism question 11 and look up Psalm 42:1–2, John 4:24, and Matthew 16:16.

  Ask, **What reasons are given to explain God as a "living God beyond all sexual distinctions"?**

  Discuss how the image of God as Father, along with other images of God, may deepen your life of faith and/or confuse it.

- Group 2: Why does the Creed speak of "God the Father"?

  Look at catechism question 12 and look up John 14:9–10, John 17: 22–24, Gal. 4:6.

  Ask, **If God is not male, why is God called "Father"?**

  Discuss the three reasons given in this catechism answer. What are other names you use to address God?

- Group 3: When we confess God as the Father of Jesus Christ, does that mean that men are to dominate women?

  Look at catechism question 13 and look up Matt. 23: 9, 11 and Gal. 3:28.

  Ask, **What kind of standard does God set with respect to misuse of power and abusive patterns of domination?** (We are to be servants to each other and exercise only power and authority that reflect God's own mercy and kindness.)

  Discuss, How are men and women called to all ministries of the church today? Is this true in all instances?

WHAT DO I THINK?

If your group is larger than twelve, you might consider breaking up into smaller groups of five to six for this portion of the discussion. Choose one or two of the following issues to discuss together. It is important to encourage the participants to enter into a dialogue with the catechism, criticizing it when they do not agree and allowing themselves to be questioned by it as well. Encourage open and free reflection during this period.

1. Invite the group to share any questions or comments they have about the catechism questions and answers. **Is there a phrase you particularly like? Is there a sentence or concept that is unclear or that you disagree with? If you could choose one phrase to hang on to, what would it be and why?**

2. Diverse Images of God

   Look again at catechism question 11. The second part of this answer focuses on several of the diverse images of God that are used in scripture. The scripture references listed below include a variety of different images for God.

   Ask for volunteers to read each scripture aloud and invite participants to call out the image for each scripture. Write a brief description for each image on the newsprint or wipe board: for example, a shepherd (Psalm 23), a nursing mother (Isaiah 49:15).

Psalm 23:1	Isaiah 42:14	Psalm 18:2
Deut. 32:18	Isaiah 49:15	Psalm 18:31
Matt. 23:37	Isaiah 66:13	Psalm 18:46

   Discuss the different images of God listed on the newsprint or wipe board. Ask, **How many different kinds of images are listed? How do these diverse images interpret different aspects of God? What other names or images would you add?**

3. The Problem of Evil

   The problem of evil is a difficult one. Ask participants to name instances of evil in the world that defy rational explanation and threaten to overcome us. List these on newsprint or wipe board.

   Discuss how the catechism and scripture passages address this issue. Read catechism question 12 responsively and invite volunteers to read Psalm 23, Job 19:25–28, and 1 Peter 1:3–5 aloud.

   Ask, What in the scripture passages and the catechism answer helps us understand God's triumph over evil? Ask, What is the "new hope" that God gives to the world?

Invite participants to share any new insights on this topic and make a list of questions that remain for further reflection.

Optional: Sing or read together "A Mighty Fortress Is Our God" (Hymn #260 in *The Presbyterian Hymnal*).

WHAT DOES THIS MEAN FOR ME TODAY?

1. God's Love and Power

   In the first article of the Apostles' Creed we affirm our faith in God who is both loving and powerful. Invite the group into a meditation on God's love and power in their lives. Give the group five to ten minutes of silence to reflect and respond to the following questions by writing in their journals.

   How have you experienced God's powerful love in your life? How have you experienced God's loving power at work in you? Where do you see God's love and power at work in the world?

   Invite participants to share with the group an insight or idea that has come from this time of reflection on God's love and power.

2. A Question about God

   Adult friends of yours confide their concern about a recent conversation with their nine-year-old daughter. "She was worried that God probably liked boys more than girls because God is a boy. We both are more comfortable imagining God as a man, and we pray to God as our Father, but this seems to be a significant issue for our daughter."

   How would you respond to your friends? How might you use insights gained from the catechism questions and scripture passages?

3. New Hope for the World

   As we have seen, it is not easy to say, "We boldly affirm that God's triumph over evil is certain" when the enormity of evil seems overwhelming. Yet, in raising Jesus Christ from the dead, God gives us "new hope" for the world.

   Invite participants to name signs of God's "new hope for the world" that they see around them. List these "new hopes" on the newsprint or wipe board next to the list of instances of evil already identified.

CLOSING

Sing together "For All the Saints" (Hymn #526 in *The Presbyterian Hymnal*, and see also catechism question and answer 10).

Close by saying the Lord's Prayer together.

The Apostles' Creed
in Question-and-Answer Form

Do you believe in God, the Father Almighty?

**I believe in God, the Father Almighty, Maker of heaven and
earth.**

Do you believe in Jesus Christ?

I believe in Jesus Christ, his only Son, our Lord.

He was conceived by the Holy Spirit, born of the Virgin Mary,

suffered under Pontius Pilate, was crucified, dead and buried.

**He descended into hell. On the third day he rose again from the
dead.**

**He ascended into heaven and is seated at the right hand of the
Father.**

He will come again to judge the living and the dead.

Do you believe in the Holy Spirit?

I believe in the Holy Spirit, the holy catholic church,

the communion of saints, the forgiveness of sins,

the resurrection of the body, and the life everlasting. Amen.

Maker of Heaven and Earth

The *Study Catechism:* Questions 15–27

Question 15. What do you believe when you say that God is "Maker of heaven and earth"?

First, that God called heaven and earth, with all that is in them, into being out of nothing simply by the power of God's Word. Second, that by that same power all things are upheld and governed in perfect wisdom, according to God's eternal purpose.

Rev. 4:11   Gen. 1:1

Heb. 11:3

Question 16. What does it mean to say that we human beings are created in the image of God?

That God created us to live together in love and freedom—with God, with one another, and with the world. Our distinctive capacities—reason, imagination, volition and so on—are given primarily for this purpose. We are created to be loving companions of others so that something of God's goodness may be reflected in our lives.

Gen. 1:26   Gen. 1:27

Question 17. What does our creation in God's image reflect about God's reality?

Our being created in and for relationship is a reflection of the Holy Trinity. In the mystery of the one God, the three divine persons—Father, Son, and Holy Spirit—live in, with, and for one another eternally in perfect love and freedom.

Luke 3:21–22   John 5:19
John 1:18   John 17:21–22

Question 18. What does our creation in God's image reflect about God's love for us?

We are created to live wholeheartedly for God. When we honor our creator as the source of all good things, we are like mirrors reflecting back the great beam of love that God shines on us. We are also created to honor God by showing love toward other human beings.

Ps. 9:1   1 John 4:11
1 John 4:7   Matt. 5:14–16

Question 19. As creatures made in God's image, what responsibility do we have for the earth?

God commands us to care for the earth in ways that reflect God's loving care for us. We are responsible for ensuring that the earth's gifts be used fairly and wisely, that no creature suffers from the abuse of what we are given, and that future generations may continue to enjoy the abundance and goodness of the earth in praise to God.

Ps. 24:1   Gen. 1:26
Ps. 89:11   Isa. 24:5
Gen. 2:15   Rom. 12:2

Question 20. Was the image of God lost when we turned from God by falling into sin?

Yes and no. Sin means that all our relations with others have become distorted and confused. Although we did not cease to be *with* God, our fellow human beings, and other creatures, we did cease to be *for* them; and although we did not lose our distinctive human capacities *completely*, we did lose the ability to use them *rightly*, especially in relation to God. Having ruined our connection with God by disobeying God's will, we are persons with hearts curved in upon ourselves. We have become slaves to the sin of which we are guilty, helpless to save ourselves, and are free, so far as freedom remains, only within the bounds of sin.

John 8:34   Rom. 1:21

Rom. 3:23   Isa. 59:1–3

Rom. 3:10

Question 21. What does it mean to say that Jesus Christ is the image of God?

Despite our turning from God, God did not turn from us, but instead sent Jesus Christ in the fullness of time to restore our broken humanity. Jesus lived completely for God, by giving himself completely for us, even to the point of dying for us. By living so completely for others, he manifested what he was: the perfect image of God. When by grace we are conformed to him through faith, our humanity is renewed according to the divine image that we lost.

Isa. 65:2   Col. 1:15

Phil. 2:8   Rom. 8:29

Question 22. What do you understand by God's providence?

That God not only preserves the world, but also continually attends to it, ruling and sustaining it with wise and benevolent care. God is concerned for every creature: "The eyes of all look to you, and you give them their food in due season. You open your hand, you satisfy the desire of every living thing" (Ps. 145:15). In particular, God provides for the world by bringing good out of evil, so that nothing evil is permitted to occur that God does not bend finally to the good. Scripture tells us, for example, how Joseph said to his brothers: "As for you, you meant evil against me; but God meant it for good, to bring it about that many people should be kept alive, as they are today" (Gen. 50:20).

Rom. 8:28   Ps. 145:17

Ps. 103:19

Question 23. What comfort do you receive by trusting in God's providence?

The eternal Father of our Lord Jesus Christ watches over me each day of my life, blessing and guiding me wherever I may be. God strengthens me when I am faithful, comforts me when discouraged or sorrowful, raises me up if I fall, and brings me at last to eternal life. Entrusting myself wholly to God's care, I receive the grace to be patient in adversity, thankful in the midst of blessing, courageous against injustice, and confident that no evil afflicts me that God will not turn to my good.

Ps. 146:9   2 Cor. 1:3–5

Isa. 58:11   Ps. 30:5

Isa. 41:10

Question 24. What difference does your faith in God's providence make when you struggle against bitterness and despair?

When I suffer harm or adversity, my faith in God's providence upholds me against bitterness and despair. It reminds me when hope disappears that my heartache and pain are contained by a larger purpose and a higher power than I can presently discern. Even in grief, shame, and loss, I can still cry out to God in lament, waiting on God to supply my needs, and to bring me healing and comfort.

Ps. 42:11   Ps. 13:1–2

2 Cor. 4:8–10   Job 7:11

Question 25. Did God need the world in order to be God?

No. God would still be God, eternally perfect and inexhaustibly rich, even if no creatures had ever been made. Without God, all created beings would simply fail to exist. Creatures can neither come into existence, nor continue, nor find fulfillment apart from God. God, however, is self-existent and self-sufficient.

Acts 17:24–25   John 5:26

John 1:16   Eph. 1:22

Question 26. Why then did God create the world?

God's decision to create the world was an act of grace. In this decision God chose to grant existence to the world simply in order to bless it. God created the world in freedom for the sake of sharing and expressing the love and beauty at the heart of God's triune being. The world was thus created to manifest God's glory and to give us eternal life in fellowship with God.

Ps. 19:1   Eph. 1:3–4

2 Cor. 3:17   John 3: 36

Ps. 67: 6–7

Theological Background

The Westminster Shorter Catechism described Creation and Providence as the "decrees of God." While this sounds today like an alarming
thing to call them, it simply means that making, ordering, and caring for
the world are expressions of God's settled and purposeful will.

CREATION

The *Study Catechism* affirms the basic Christian recognition that the
world is good because it is the creation of the good God, and God has
called it good. Scholars of the relation between science and theology,
such as Herbert Butterfield and Thomas F. Torrance, have pointed out
that this basic conviction that the universe is a good creation lies at the
root of the development of modern science. A world that is understood
to be good is therefore worth our time and effort to examine and seek
understanding. If the world were thought to be evil, or to be capricious
rather than law-abiding, no one would think to try to understand it.

However, the goodness of creation only becomes apparent when
we have recognized that this world is not all there is. If Carl Sagan's
hymnic and hopeless claim that "the cosmos is all there is, all there
ever was, and all there ever will be" were true, we would never be able
to discern it as a "cosmos" (an ordered existence) at all. Apart from our
understanding of the universe as a creation and not as a random hap-
pening, the tragic and random destruction of beauty and of life that

occurs would obscure the ordered character of the universe. This reality is nowhere more clear than in the anxious fretting over correct ritual in pagan religion, in order to manipulate the energies and processes of the universe, trying to order the chaos of life.

The *Study Catechism* focuses closely on the issue of what it means for us to be made "in the image of God." Everyone who wishes to speak in the mode of Christian theology about what it means to be human must come to terms with this phrase. In Genesis 1:26, God says, "Let us make humankind in our own image. . . ," and in the next verse we are told, "So God made humankind in his own image; male and female he created them." The *Study Catechism* follows the clue in this verse ("male and female") and affirms that the image of God is the capacity for relationships. Some have suggested that the image of God is reason, imagination, or will, but the catechism points out that all these are aspects of the image of God, which is best summarized in the affirmation that we are created with the capacity for relationships.

The reality of sin in human life, however, means that, in the catechism's words, "All our relations with others have become distorted and confused" (question 20). Sin means that even though human beings remain human, we are no longer able on our own to live for God or to take to heart those around us. It is not merely that we cannot reach our fullest potential, but rather that we cannot live at all the kind of life God intended for us. Only Jesus Christ has done that. While it is said in scripture that we are made *in* the image of God, the Bible also teaches that Jesus Christ *is* the image of God in which we are made (Col. 1:15; Rom. 8:29). We look to Jesus Christ not only to learn what God is like, but also to learn who we are meant to be.

PROVIDENCE

The providence of God is God's activity of "providing, ordering, and caring" for the creation.[3] The doctrine of providence is beautifully summarized in a classic prayer at mealtime, which asks God to "help us look to thee for all our good, and receive it from thy hand with thanksgiving." We also acknowledge God's providence when we say in the Lord's Prayer, "Give us this day our daily bread." However, our faith in God's providence goes beyond looking to God for bodily provision. Faith in God's providence orients our lives to God, through the recognition that everything we have and everything that occurs reflects in some way the will of God. The sense in which this is true is often clearer in hindsight than in the midst of crisis.

The Distinction of Creator and Creation

Questions 25–27 of the catechism address the important but often overlooked issue of the distinction between God and the universe. Although God chooses not to be without the universe, without the universe God would still be God. The creation is not part of God; for example, it is not "God's body," as has sometimes been said. Unlike pagan divinities, which are personified aspects of worldly existence and are not distinct from the universe, God is free from any need to compete with us over the allocation of rights and resources. This is how God is free to have mercy on us. If God were not distinct from the world, justice would be God's only option.

Questions about miracles, the resurrection, or the virgin birth fade in difficulty when we place them alongside the distinction between God and creation. The most fundamental problem Christian faith presents to the unbeliever is the idea that there is an absolute qualitative difference between God and everything that is not God. This is the point about Christian faith that is truly counter-intuitive, and indeed impossible to think through completely. As philosophers such as Hegel and Wittgenstein have pointed out, in order to think a boundary we have to be able to think both sides of it, and in the distinction between God and creation, this is what we cannot do. We cannot think this distinction from God's side, only from our own, the side of finitude.[4]

Only when this important distinction is held is it possible to say, as we often do to children, that God is everywhere. If we blur the distinction between Creator and Creation, then to say that God is everywhere is to imply that God's being is dispersed throughout the universe. But God's presence is an *act* of God, God's decision, not passive dispersion. To say God is everywhere is to affirm that God can act freely and personally in any place, at any time, in any life.

Christianity and Science

There is no general agreement today about how the relationship between Christianity and contemporary science should be understood. Some things are, however, clear.

For one, it is important that we keep a sense of proportion. The catechism affirms that "Nothing basic to the Christian faith contradicts the findings of modern science, nor does anything basic to modern science contradict the Christian faith" (question 27). It is true that in light of what we know scientifically about the ordering of the universe, certain things that are reported in scripture, apparently as events, are improbable (which is not the same as saying they did not happen!). One important question is whether the historicity of such events is "basic to the Christian faith." As John H. Leith has observed, to claim that the total integrity of Christian faith hangs on whether an ax head floated or a serpent talked lacks seriousness.[5] An even more important issue, though, is whether the reported events are what such passages are actually *about*. Few if any such passages are attempting to communicate to us a theory about the mechanical functioning of the universe. We must, then, not allow our science to rush us past the possibility of sense and value in such problematic passages of scripture.

Second, it is important for us to remember that, in company with many excellent scientists, Christianity claims that there are limits to scientific knowledge. For example, science is limited in that it can never answer the question, Why is there a universe, rather than nothing? Paul Tillich phrased this question helpfully in the form, Why is the world not *not*? Science also cannot answer the question why the universe has the particular members it does, rather than others.[6] In other words, Why are there horses and bulls and goats, but not unicorns or minotaurs or fauns? Christians, following the witness of scripture, understand that the answer is to be found in the creative intention of God.

Thus it is simply not the case that every truth about the world can be quantified and verified empirically. In fact, only a few can be, and many of those are ultimately trivial. Analytical reason is only one arrow in our intellectual quiver; we are equipped by God with other ways of discerning truth, such as imagination and intuition, filtered by the witness of scripture, which is the standard of our faith. G. K. Chesterton, C. S. Lewis, and J. R. R. Tolkien were three emphatically Christian, intellectually rigorous writers of the modern era who all understood that there are truths that can only be learned from fairy tales, truths about which scientists as scientists are completely in the dark. Such Christians as these have understood with greater clarity than most that though modern science is highly impressive, there are genuine and vitally important truths to which it will never lead us.

Some of these truths are ethical. Marilynne Robinson has made this point with great force: "The modern fable is that science exposed religion as a delusion and more or less supplanted it. But science cannot serve in the place of religion because it cannot generate an ethics or a morality. It can give us no reason to prefer a child to a dog, or to choose honorable poverty over fraudulent wealth. It can give us no grounds for preferring what is excellent to what is sensationalistic."[7]

For Further Study

An excellent recent book on sin is Cornelius Plantinga, *Not the Way It's Supposed to Be: A Breviary of Sin* (Grand Rapids: Wm. B. Eerdmans Publishing Co., 1995).

Robert Sokolowski gives a masterful account of the distinction between God and the universe in *The God of Faith and Reason* (Washington, D.C.: Catholic University of America Press, 1995).

The area of science and theology is overflowing with books of widely varying quality. An excellent and brief starting point is Thomas F. Torrance's slim volume *Preaching Christ Today* (Grand Rapids: Wm. B. Eerdmans Publishing Co., 1994). Everything Torrance has written on this subject is worth reading. Diogenes Allen also deals lucidly with this issue in his *Christian Belief in a Postmodern World* (Louisville, Ky.: Westminster/John Knox Press, 1989). For a different perspective, in which theology is instructed concerning "the God in whom it is possible today to believe," from the viewpoint of British natural theology, see Arthur Peacocke, *Theology for a Scientific Age* (Philadelphia: Fortress Press, 1993).

Chesterton's chapter "The Ethics of Elfland," in his book (originally published in 1905) *Orthodoxy: The Romance of Faith* (New York: Doubleday, 1990), is an excellent place to start exploring the idea of imagination as a carrier of truth. Tolkien's famous essay "On Fairy Stories," which has been reprinted often, is a helpful place to find this idea applied to the Christian gospel. As of this writing it is in print in *The Tolkien Reader* (New York: Ballantine Books, Inc., 1986).

PREPARATION AND MATERIALS NEEDED

- Read over carefully the background material and the lesson plan.
- Make decisions where necessary about optional activities, whether to divide into small groups, etc.
- Provide nametags and markers.
- Have newsprint or a wipe board available.
- Provide a VCR and monitor and a video depicting the Genesis account of creation. (See suggestions given under "Getting Started" on page 43.) Optional.

- Write instructions for Forced Choice Exercise (page 44) on newsprint or poster board.

Lesson Plan—Session 3: Maker of Heaven and Earth. Questions 15–27

WELCOME AND REVIEW

Greet everyone and be sure that they know each other. Provide nametags if needed.

Review lessons 1 and 2 by reading *Study Catechism* questions 1 and 7 in the *Student Guide* on page 18. Ask one person to ask the questions and participants to read the answers together.

> *Question 1. What is God's purpose for your life?*
>
> God wills that I should live by the grace of the Lord Jesus Christ, for the love of God, and in the communion of the Holy Spirit.
>
> *Question 7. What do you believe when you confess your faith in "God the Father Almighty"?*
>
> That God is a God of love, and that God's love is powerful beyond measure.

Ask for questions or reflections about material studied in previous lessons.

Refer the group to the chart outlining the *Study Catechism*'s discussion of the first article in the Apostles' Creed used last week. Make additional copies if needed or write the outline on the wipe board or on newsprint for the class to see.

The First Article of the Apostles' Creed	Question 6
I believe in God the Father Almighty	7
God's Love and Power	8–10
Meaning of "God the Father"	11–13
God's Powerful Love vs. Evil	14
Maker of Heaven and Earth	15
Created in God's Image	16–21
God's Providence and Care	22–24
Creation as God's Act of Grace	25–26
Creation and Modern Science	27

Tell the group that this week the class will focus on the second part of the first article, "God, the Maker of Heaven and Earth," and themes of creation and providence.

GETTING STARTED

Choose one of the following activities:

1. Have participants close their eyes and visualize in their minds' eye the biblical narrative of Creation. Read aloud Genesis 1:1–2:3 with expression. Following the reading, invite participants to gather in groups of two or three to share what part of the story was most striking. Ask the group for reactions to the experience: **What did God create? How did God respond to the creation? What impressed you most? What new insights occurred as a result of this experience?**

2. A video presentation can also bring the story of creation to life. Consider using "The New Media Bible" videotape of Genesis 1:1–2:3 or the videotape or audio tape of "God's Trombones" by James Weldon Johnson (many presbytery resource centers have copies available for loan). Preview the tape and set it for the portion you want to show. Ask the group for reactions to the experience: **What did God create? How did God respond to the creation? What impressed you most? What new insights occurred as a result of this experience?**

Remind them of the three basic steps that will be followed in the session:

What does the church confess?

What do I think?

What does this mean for me?

WHAT DOES THE CHURCH CONFESS?

1. Read *Study Catechism* questions 15–21 responsively. Have one person read the questions and the rest of the group respond with the answers. Direct class members to page 18 in the *Student Guide*.

2. Created in God's Image

The *Study Catechism* questions 16–19 focuses on different aspects of what it means to be created in God's image. Let's take a closer look using the catechism and scripture references.

Divide into three groups. (If you have fewer than six participants, do this activity as one group. If you have a very large class, divide into more than three groups and assign some or all of the questions to more than one group.)

Group 1: Created in God's Image
> Look at question 16 and Genesis 1:26–27.
> Who is created in God's image? Are there any prerequisites?
> What are we created to be and do?

Group 2: Reflecting God our Creator
> Look at question 17 and John 5:19 and John 17:21–22.
> How are we a reflection of the Holy Trinity?

Group 3: Reflecting God's Love to Others
> Look at question 18 and 1 John 4:7, 11 and Matthew 5:14–16.
> How do we reflect God's love for us to others?

Bring the groups back together and invite a spokesperson from each group to share briefly what they came up with.

3. The Providence of God

Read *Study Catechism* question 22 responsively from the *Student Guide*, page 22. As a group, develop a working definition of providence by noting the different verbs in this catechism answer.

Ask, **According to this answer what are the different roles and actions that God takes in caring for the Creation?** List these for all to see.

Ask, **What examples of God "bringing good out of evil" and "bending evil to good" can we find in scripture? What examples in life experiences?**

4. Forced Choice Exercise

Designate one side of the room for question 23 and another side for question 24. Ask class members to choose which question on God's providence they want to discuss in more detail. Then move to the appropriate side and discuss the catechism question in groups of two or three. Write instructions on a sheet of newsprint before class and post it on the wall.

Question 23 **Receiving Comfort in God's Providence**

Read the question silently and identify words or phrases that are most meaningful to you. Share them with the group. Ask someone to read Isaiah 58:11 aloud. Discuss examples of how the scripture reading connects with the catechism response.

Question 24 **God's Providence in Times of Struggle and Despair**

Read the question silently and identify words or phrases that are most meaningful to you and share them with the group. Ask someone to read 2 Corinthians 4:7–10 aloud. Discuss examples of how the scripture reading connects with the catechism response.

Call the group back together as a whole. Say, One of the great hymns of the church that deals with this issue of providence in struggle is "If Thou but Trust in God to Guide Thee" (#282 in *The Presbyterian Hymnal*). Invite the group to read or sing this hymn, noting the words of comfort it provides.

WHAT DO I THINK?

If your group is larger than twelve, you might consider breaking up into smaller groups of five or six for this portion of the discussion. Remember, it is important to encourage the participants to enter into a dialogue with the catechism, criticizing it when they do not agree and allowing themselves to be questioned by it as well. In short, encourage open and free reflection during this period.

1. Invite the group to share any questions or comments they have about the catechism questions and answers that have been discussed in this lesson. Ask, **Is there a phrase you particularly like? Is there a sentence or concept that is unclear or that you disagree with? If you could choose one phrase to hang on to, what would it be and why?**

2. Ask, **Has anyone here ever wondered why God chose to create the world? What are some of the reasons you thought of or heard from others?** Invite participants in groups to share ideas.

   One reason sometimes given for the creation of the world is that God was lonely and created the world and its creatures to keep God company and to make God complete and whole. **Did God create the world to benefit and fulfill God's being?**

3. Read catechism questions 25 and 26. **What are the reasons given here for God's creation of the world?** (to reveal God's glory, to share in God's love and freedom, and to give us eternal life in fellowship with God). **How do you understand creation as an act of God's grace rather than God's need?**

Ask someone to read the final sentence of question 26 aloud. Invite participants to give examples in their lives when they have seen God's glory in the world God created or shared in God's love and freedom.

WHAT DOES THIS MEAN FOR ME TODAY?

1. Spend some time in silent reflection on God's providence, goodness, and grace. List some of the ways you see, feel, and experience God's providence, goodness, and grace. Invite three or four participants to share an example from their lists with the group.

2. Imagine that a friend of yours who is a college freshman stops by to see you during Christmas vacation. She was an active member of the high school youth ministry group when you were an adult advisor. She confides that she's having a difficult time reconciling her Christian beliefs with what she is learning in her science courses. She is frank to say that Christianity sometimes seems rather primitive and outdated compared with the findings of modern science.

   How would you use question 27 in the *Study Catechism* to help her discern both the contributions of modern science, as well as its limitations in dealing with matters of faith?

3. Catechism question 21 reminds us that "as creatures who are made in God's image," we have responsibility to care for the earth in a manner that "reflects God's loving care for us." Invite participants to give some specific instances of how we are NOT caring for the earth fairly and wisely. Identify specific ways we can make a commitment to taking care of the earth for future generations.

CLOSING

Comment that we have now finished the article of the Apostles' Creed. Next week we will begin the second article on Jesus Christ. As we say together the Apostles' Creed, think carefully about the meaning of the words.

Close by saying the Apostles' Creed together and the Lord's Prayer.

SESSION 4

Who Is Jesus Christ?

The *Study Catechism:* Questions 28–41

Question 28. What is the second article of the Apostles' Creed?

"And I believe in Jesus Christ, his only Son, our Lord. He was conceived by the Holy Spirit, born of the Virgin Mary, suffered under Pontius Pilate, was crucified, dead and buried. He descended into hell. On the third day he rose again from the dead. He ascended into heaven and is seated at the right hand of the Father. He will come again to judge the living and the dead.

Question 29. What do you believe when you confess your faith in Jesus Christ as "God's only Son"?

That Jesus Christ is a unique person who was sent to do a unique work.

Luke 3:21–22   John 1:14

Luke 12:49–50

Question 30: How do you understand the uniqueness of Jesus Christ?

No one else will ever be God incarnate. No one else will ever die for the sins of the world. Only Jesus Christ is such a person, only he could do such a work, and he in fact has done it.

Isa. 53:5   Col. 1:15–20

John 1:29

Question 31. What do you affirm when you confess your faith in Jesus Christ as "our Lord"?

That having been raised from the dead he reigns with compassion and justice over all things in heaven and on earth, especially over those who confess him by faith; and that by loving and serving him above all else, I give glory and honor to God.

1 Cor. 15:3–4   Eph. 1:20–23

Rev. 11:15   Phil. 2:9–11

Question 32. What do you affirm when you say he was "conceived by the Holy Spirit and born of the Virgin Mary"?

First, that being born of a woman, Jesus was truly a human being. Second, that our Lord's incarnation was a holy and mysterious event, brought about solely by free divine grace surpassing any human possibilities. Third, that from the very beginning of his life on earth, he was set apart by his unique origin for the sake of accomplishing our salvation.

Luke 1:31   Heb. 2:14

Luke 1:35   Phil. 2:5–7

Question 33. What is the significance of affirming that Jesus is truly God?

Only God can properly deserve worship. Only God can reveal to us who God is. And only God can save us from our sins. Being truly God, Jesus meets these conditions. He is the proper object of our worship, the self-revelation of God, and the Savior of the world.

Matt. 11:27   1 John 4:14

John 20:28

Question 34. What is the significance of affirming that Jesus is also truly a human being?

Being truly human, Jesus entered fully into our fallen situation and overcame it from within. By his pure obedience, he lived a life of unbroken unity with God, even to the point of accepting a violent death. As sinners at war with grace, this is precisely the kind of life we fail to live. When we accept him by faith, he removes our disobedience and clothes us with his perfect righteousness.

Heb. 2:17–18   Heb. 5:8–9

Heb. 4:15   Rom. 5:19

Question 35. How can Jesus be truly God and yet also truly human at the same time?

The mystery of Jesus Christ's divine-human unity passes our understanding; only faith given by the Holy Spirit enables us to affirm it. When Holy Scripture depicts Jesus as someone with divine power, status, and authority, it presupposes his humanity. And when it depicts him as someone with human weakness, neediness, and mortality, it presupposes his deity. We cannot understand how this should be, but we can trust that the God who made heaven and earth is free to become God incarnate and thus to be God with us in this wonderful and awe-inspiring way.

Mark 1:27	Luke 22:44
Mark 4:41	Job 5:9
Matt. 28:18	

Question 36. How did God use the people of Israel to prepare the way for the coming of Jesus?

God made a covenant with Israel, promising that God would be their light and their salvation, that they would be God's people, and that through them all the peoples of the earth would be blessed. Therefore, no matter how often Israel turned away from God, God still cared for them and acted on their behalf. In particular, God sent them prophets, priests, and kings. Each of these was "anointed" by God's Spirit—prophets, to declare God's word; priests, to make sacrifice for the people's sins; and kings, to rule justly in the fear of God, upholding the poor and needy, and defending the people from their enemies.

Gen. 17:3–4	1 Peter 2:9–10
Gen. 12:1–3	Zech. 1:6
Ex. 6:4–5	Lev. 5:6
Gal. 3:14	Ps. 72:1, 4
Jer. 30:22	

Question 37. Was the covenant with Israel an everlasting covenant?

Yes. With the coming of Jesus the covenant with Israel was expanded and confirmed. By faith in him Gentiles were welcomed into the covenant. This throwing open of the gates confirmed the promise that through Israel God's blessing would come to all peoples. Although for the most part Israel has not accepted Jesus as the Messiah, God has not rejected Israel. God still loves

Israel, and God is their hope, "for the gifts and the calling of God are irrevocable" (Rom. 11:29). The God who has reached out to unbelieving Gentiles will not fail to show mercy to Israel as the people of the everlasting covenant.

Isa. 61:8   2 Sam. 23:5

Jer. 31:3   Rom. 11:29

Question 38. Why was the title "Christ," which means "anointed one," applied to Jesus?

Jesus Christ was the definitive prophet, priest, and king. All of the Lord's anointed in Israel anticipated and led finally to him. In assuming these offices, Jesus not only transformed them, but also realized the purpose of Israel's election for the sake of the world.

2 Cor. 1:20   Luke 4:16–19

Acts 10:37–38

Question 39. How did Jesus Christ fulfill the office of prophet?

He was God's Word to a dying and sinful world; he embodied the love he proclaimed. His life, death, and resurrection became the great Yes that continues to be spoken despite how often we have said No. When we receive this Word by faith, Christ himself enters our hearts, that he may dwell in us forever, and we in him.

Acts 3:20, 22   Eph. 3:17

John 1:18

Question 40. How did Jesus Christ fulfill the office of priest?

He was the Lamb of God that took away the sin of the world; he became our priest and sacrifice in one. Confronted by our hopelessness in sin and death, Christ interceded by offering himself—his entire person and work—in order to reconcile us to God.

Heb. 4:14   Heb. 2:17

John 1:29   Eph. 1:7

Question 41. How did Jesus Christ fulfill the office of king?

He was the Lord who took the form of a servant; he perfected royal power in weakness. With no sword but the sword

of righteousness, and no power but the power of love, Christ
defeated sin, evil, and death by reigning from the cross.

| John 19:19 | 1 Cor. 1:25 |
| Phil. 2:5–8 | John 12:32 |

Theological Background

THE UNIQUENESS OF JESUS CHRIST

The Creed's affirmation that Jesus Christ is God's "only Son" follows the biblical witness by pointing to the uniqueness of God's incarnation in Jesus Christ. As the catechism puts it, "No one else will ever
be God incarnate" (question 30). Karl Barth has pointed out that bad
theology has shaded over into more mundane evils, such as demonic
politics, when the church has treated Jesus Christ as something other
than God the Son living a human life. Jesus Christ is not, as Barth put
it, "a divine intermediate being" suspended indefinitely between
heaven and earth, one of many equally optional steps to knowing God.
To understand Jesus Christ in that way is at heart a form of polytheism
(belief in many gods), because it makes Christ one (lower) divinity,
and the God to whom he leads another. Such a weakening of the integral connection between the inner life of the Triune God and the incarnation of God in Jesus Christ led directly to the theology of the Nazi
"German Christian" movement in the 1930s.[8] However, as many
scholars have pointed out, the uniqueness of Jesus Christ remains the
scandal of the gospel in the postmodern world, which demands that
there must be many incarnations of God. Like the apostle Paul, we
confess the uniqueness of Christ in a culture that sees such faith as
foolishness and a stumbling block.

When in the creed we confess that Christ is not only God the Son,
but also "our Lord," we apply the uniqueness of Christ ethically in our
own lives. As the catechism puts it, Jesus Christ, "reigns . . . over all
things in heaven and on earth, especially over those who confess him
by faith" (question 31). Dallas Willard, in a valuable article on discipleship, has proposed that Christ is the Master to whom we have ap-
prenticed ourselves, and living under his Lordship means learning "to
live my life as he would lead it if he were I."[9]

Let us note well that the Lordship of Jesus Christ in human life is
first of all Lordship over the church, "those who confess him by faith,
and only in the second place do I as an individual give glory and

honor to God through loving and serving him above all else. The fact that Christ becomes the Lord of my whole life is not something that I can have alone," but only in the Body of Christ.[10]

THE PERSON OF CHRIST

Under the heading of Christ's divine origin and birth to Mary, the *Study Catechism,* in keeping with the Apostles' Creed, deals with the issue of Christ's two natures united in a single person. The ancient theologians associated Christ's conception by the Holy Spirit with his divine nature and the motherhood of Mary as the statement of his true humanity. In contrast to our modern tendency to associate it with Christ's divinity, the virgin conception of Christ was historically always denied by those who wished to deny his true humanity, and affirmed by those who wished to affirm that he was human as we are.

With characteristic precision, the catechism speaks of Christ's being *truly* human and *truly* God (questions 33 and 34). Often one sees this expressed as "fully human and fully God." Although it may seem a small point, to speak of Christ's "full" humanity and divinity evokes an unnecessarily confusing idea that we are speaking of quantities of divine and human stuff. It is true that the idea of fullness may remind us that Christ's divinity and humanity are each complete and not partial. However, the doctrine of Christ's two natures is not about quantities or percentages, but about genuineness. Jesus' divinity as well as his humanity are each genuine and complete; they are not approximations. He is truly God, which means he is God in the way the Father is God, only he is not the Father; and he is truly human, thus human in the way we are human, only he is not alienated from the Father by sin.

Finally, no discussion of Christ's two natures is complete without the third affirmation that he is a single integrated self (question 35). He is truly God and truly human in one person, one self who can meaningfully say "I". This final, crucial affirmation, which was traditionally called the doctrine of the hypostatic union, has unfortunately become rather scarce in ecclesiastical summaries of Christian doctrine. However, it is crucial because this, too, is an affirmation of Christ's uniqueness. He is God living a particular life as a single, human self, and not merely a spiritual model to inspire us to give God our best.

COVENANT AND THE OFFICES OF CHRIST

God deals with us by covenant. There have been many understandings of this idea in the history of Christian thought, and even the Reformed tradition, which has made lively use of it, is not of one mind. There are several points we can understand with assurance, though.

First, a covenant is not unlike a contract. It is, in a manner of speaking, a "deal." In a covenant relation, two parties agree together on certain terms of their relationship. If the parties are equal, they negotiate those terms. In the case of God's covenants with Israel and the Church, God has specified gracious and yet demanding terms that we accept. In some forms of covenant theology, the vital relational aspect of the covenant was lost, leaving only a legalistic contract allowing both parties coolly to demand specific performance. Although there are biblical passages that make use of legal analogies, this legalism is not the biblical view of God's covenant relations with us.

Second, it is clear that there are at least two foundational covenants in scripture, which correspond roughly to the two parts of the Christian Bible, the Old and New Testaments. (This should not be confused with a simplistic division between Law in the Old Testament and Gospel in the New.) *Testament* and *Covenant* are synonymous. Both can be used to translate the Hebrew *berith* and the Greek *diatheke*, the biblical words for this concept. Scripture makes it very clear in passages such as Romans 9–11 that the covenant with Israel, even though it is in a sense "old" is nevertheless still in force and is fulfilled rather than superseded by the "new" covenant in Christ (question 37).

Jesus Christ is the mediator of the new covenant between God and the church, and he mediates this covenant through his "threefold office" of prophet, priest, and king. As the catechism reminds us, God has always maintained the covenant with his people through such "anointed" servants. In Jesus Christ, the traditions of prophecy, priesthood, and theocratic monarchy reach their fulfillment.

Jesus Christ is the definitive and final prophet in that, in contrast to the prophets of the Old Covenant to whom the word of God came, he is the Word of God incarnate (John 1:1–18). Jesus is the definitive and final priest in that, in contrast to priests of the Old Covenant who repeatedly sacrificed animals for the sin of the people and interceded for them with God, he willingly sacrificed *himself*, even though he was himself guilty of nothing, to reconcile us once and for all to God (Heb. 5:1–10). Now, according to scripture, we have access to God directly through Christ as our priest. Jesus Christ is the definitive and final king in that, in contrast to the kings of the Old Covenant whose authority was based, humanly speaking, upon the effective deployment of military and economic power, Christ rules by exercising the love and judgment of God.

For Further Study

On the problem of maintaining a robust Christianity in a pluralistic culture, the works of Bishop Lesslie Newbigin are full of insight. For a highly nuanced treatment of the possibility of high Christology in a religiously pluralistic situation, see his *Finality of Christ* (London: SCM Press, 1969). The general problem is treated magisterially in *The Gospel in a Pluralist Society* (Grand Rapids: Wm. B. Eerdmans Publishing Co., 1989).

For a clear and helpful overview of the doctrine of the person of Christ as it developed historically, see J. N. D. Kelly, *Early Christian Doctrines* (San Francisco: Harper & Row, 1978), 280–395. The very living end of Christological studies is Aloys Grillmeier's three-volume *Christ in Christian Tradition* (Philadelphia: Fortress, 1975), which will tell most people far more than they want to know, but is indispensable for detailed Christological study.

Exactly what covenant theology is and has been is vigorously debated among scholars of Reformed Orthodoxy and Puritanism today, and no one treatment has broad authority. One original source where several strands of covenant thinking meet is in Francis Turretin, *Institutes of Elenctic Theology* (Phillipsburg, N.J.: Presbyterian & Reformed, 1992).

Preparation and Materials Needed

- Read over carefully the background material and the lesson plan.
- Make decisions where necessary about optional activities, whether to divide into small groups, etc.
- Provide nametags and markers.
- Post artwork around the room depicting Jesus. Try to select artwork representing a variety of cultures and styles. If you do not have access to such prints through your church or presbytery resource center, obtain a copy of the March 22, 1999, issue of *Newsweek*, which featured an article entitled "2000 Years of Jesus" accompanied by a wide variety of artistic depictions of Jesus.
- Write the outline of the second article of the Apostles' Creed (found on page 57) on poster or newsprint.
- Have newsprint or a wipe board available.

Lesson Plan—Session 4: Who Is Jesus Christ? Questions 28–41

WELCOME AND REVIEW

Greet everyone as they come in. Be sure that everyone knows each other.

Provide nametags if a large group.

Review lessons 1, 2, and 3 by asking questions 1, 7, and 15 from the catechism and having the class repeat the answers together:

> *Question 1. What is God's purpose for your life?*
>
> God wills that I should live by the grace of the Lord Jesus Christ, for the love of God, and in the communion of the Holy Spirit.
>
> *Question 7. What do you believe when you confess your faith in "God the Father Almighty"?*
>
> That God is a God of love, and that God's love is powerful beyond measure.
>
> *Question 15. What do you believe when you say that God is "Maker of heaven and earth"?*
>
> First, that God called heaven and earth, with all that is in them, into being out of nothing simply by the power of God's Word. Second, that by that same power all things are upheld and governed in perfect wisdom, according to God's eternal purpose.

Ask for questions or reflections about material studied in previous sessions.

GETTING STARTED

Read question 28: the second article of the Apostles' Creed. We will spend two weeks on this portion of the Apostles' Creed.

Introductory Remarks

This week and next we cover some of the most important material in the Apostles' Creed and the *Study Catechism,* for it deals with the person and work of Jesus Christ. For all of us, those who are new to the church or those who have been involved in the church all our lives, understanding who Jesus is remains at the heart of the Christian life.

The New Testament tells us that Jesus asked his disciples, "Who do *you* say that I am?" (Matthew 16:15) He continues to pose this question to those who would be his disciples today. In fact, when you join the church in a few weeks, the first and most important question you will be asked is: Do you believe that Jesus Christ is your Lord and Savior? What is at stake in saying, "I do"? This week and next we will be studying together what the catechism has to teach us about this question.

Opening Activity

1. To get a feel for the many different ways Christians have understood the significance of Jesus, let's look at some Christian art that depicts him in different ways.

   Point to art already posted around the room depicting Jesus in different ways. Ask the participants to move around the room and jot down some of the differences in the ways the pictures depict Jesus.

   After a few moments, ask them to stand next to the picture that comes closest to their understanding of Jesus. Invite them to discuss with others standing next to that picture why they chose it. Invite those standing alone to join others.

2. Invite the group to sit back down and to share in "popcorn" fashion (quickly and with few words) various words or phrases that describe some of the different ways Jesus is depicted in the pictures.

   Remind them of the three basic steps that will be followed in the session:

   What does the church confess?

   What do I think?

   What does this mean for me?

WHAT DOES THE CHURCH CONFESS?

1. An Overview of the Second Article as Treated in the *Study Catechism*

   Provide the participants with a brief overview to the *Study Catechism*'s treatment of the second article of the Apostles' Creed. By and large, it covers topics as they appear in the creed, expanding different themes at points. Consider writing the following outline on poster paper:

The Second Article of the Apostles' Creed   **Question 28**

Remind the participants that we will be focusing on questions 28–41 today, and 42–52 next week. Today, thus, we are focusing on the uniqueness of Jesus as truly human and divine and the nature of his work as prophet, priest, and king.

2. A Discussion: The Uniqueness of Jesus Christ. Questions 29–35

Read questions 29–30 responsively. Call attention to the accent on the uniqueness of the person and work of Christ. Discuss, using questions like these:

- **What does answer 30 name as the most important dimensions of Christ's uniqueness?** (Jesus is God incarnate and he alone dies for our sins.)

- Across the centuries the church has described Jesus' coming in terms of the doctrine of the Incarnation. Let's see how the catechism treats this doctrine. Invite the group to read silently questions 32–35, focusing on the word "truly." After they've done so, ask: **Suppose the word "truly" were to provide you with the key to this doctrine. How would you define it?** (Jesus was both truly human and truly God.)

- Why is it important to affirm both parts of this doctrine? What happens if only one part gets affirmed? Is it possible to think "too little" of Jesus, affirming only his humanity? What about "too much," affirming only his divinity?

- Thinking "too little" of Jesus

  Can you think of examples in our society today in which individuals or groups affirm only the humanity of Jesus? What about inside the church? What happens, for example, when we think of Jesus exclusively as a moral example for Christian living today? What gets lost?

- Point out that answer 33 notes that God alone can save us from our sins and that, in fact, Jesus has done so. What happens when we forget that we cannot save ourselves? Sometimes this is known as "works righteousness," the idea that we can earn God's favor through our own good works. Frequently, this leads to a form of legalism, as found in the response of the Pharisees to Jesus.

  Are there forms of Christian legalism present in the church today? What forms do they take? How do they distort the important teaching that "only God can save us from our sins"? (You may want to save these questions for later if you choose topic 1 under "What Do I Think?")

- Thinking "too much" of Jesus

  On the other hand, what happens when we think of Jesus solely in terms of his divinity? When we remove him from real life, do we run the risk of turning his life into a kind of fairytale that is nice to think about on Sunday but has nothing to do with our world and its problems?

  Ask the group to turn ahead a bit in the Study Catechism and look at the first part of answer 42. Here, Jesus' suffering is portrayed as an act of divine solidarity with all persons who suffer unjustly at the hands of worldly power. What are some examples of persons who suffer unjustly today? Why does the Son of God in his human, earthly ministry identify with those who suffer in these ways?

- Question 44 describes the creed's affirmation of Jesus' descent into Hell as pointing to the extent to which Christ suffered for our sakes and in solidarity with those who suffer unjustly. It uses the phrase "agony of abandonment by God." **What might this mean? Have you ever felt abandoned by God? Have you known anyone who felt this way? Is this sort of absolute separation from God a good definition of Hell? Is it possible to experience in some measure Hell on earth?**

3. A Discussion of the Threefold Office of Christ: Questions 36–41

The Reformed tradition out of which the Presbyterian Church emerged has traditionally described the work of Christ in terms of his threefold office. This goes back to John Calvin and was one of his most important contributions to the Western tradition of Christian theology. The *Study Catechism* uses this framework, not only to draw on a central theological theme of our tradition, but also because many people today continue to find it a useful way of summarizing the three most important aspects of Jesus Christ's work as God incarnate. The catechism takes up this theme in its treatment of Christ's conception by the Holy Spirit and birth of the Virgin Mary. Remind the group that from the beginning, God prepared the way for the coming of the Son, not only in the immediate events surrounding Jesus' birth, but also in the longer history of God's dealings with Israel.

- Ask the group to read responsively questions 36–41. Discuss initially by asking: **What does the term** *covenant* **mean? What are some contemporary examples of covenants?** (marriage, baptism) **How is a covenant like a contract? How is it different?**

- If you have time, the group might look up passages dealing with the covenant like Genesis 12:1–4; Exodus 6:1–8, and Jeremiah 30:22. God's covenant was renewed in the New Testament with the new covenant in Jesus Christ. Consider reading 1 Peter 2:9–10.

- The *Study Catechism* teaches us that God prepared the way for the coming of Jesus through God's covenant with Israel. **What three groups of leaders were sent by God to help Israel keep the covenant? Why was it important that they were anointed by the Spirit?**

- Let's explore the contribution each group made to the life of Israel by studying scripture. Divide into three groups. Each group looks at a different office in ancient Israel. Write the questions and scripture passages on newspaper or photocopy this section so that each group has a copy.

Group 1: Prophets

Look at the Old Testament role of prophet in 1 Samuel 3:19–20. What are the defining characteristics of a prophet as portrayed in this passage?

Examine Jesus' fulfillment of this office as described in Ephesians 3:14–19, 1 John 4:13, Acts 3:17–26.

After completing this task, the group should look at question 39. Discuss.

Group 2: Priests

Look at the Old Testament role of priest as found in Exodus 28:1–5. What was the role of the priest at the time of Aaron?

How did Jesus fulfill the priestly office? Read John 1:29 and Hebrews 4:14, 2:17.

Discuss together the answer to question 40.

Group 3: Kings

Look at the Old Testament role of king as found in 1 Samuel 16:1–13. What was the role of the king as seen through the greatest king of Israel, King David?

How did Jesus fulfill the royal office? Read and discuss John 19:19, Philippians 2:5–8, 1 Corinthians 1:25, and John 12:32.

Then discuss together question 41. How is Jesus as king different from our cultural definition of a king?

Total group sharing

Invite representatives of each group to report on the findings of their group. As a group, reflect together on why these three offices, taken together, serve as a nice summary of the most important aspects of Jesus' work as the Son of God.

WHAT DO I THINK?

Choose one of the following topics for further reflection. Remember, it is important to encourage the participants to enter into a dialogue with the catechism, criticizing it when they do not agree and allowing themselves to be questioned by it as well. In short, encourage open and free reflection during this period.

Topic One: Christian Pharisees

The *Study Catechism* makes a great deal of the uniqueness of Christ, teaching that God alone in Christ can save us from our sins. Sometimes, Christians do not seem to think this is true, acting like they can save themselves from their sins through their good works. Just as the Pharisees opposed Jesus in their legalism, so, too, do many Christians seem to behave in a legalistic fashion like modern-day Pharisees.

- What might Pharisaic Christianity look like? Are some of the leading figures in American Christianity today really closer to the Pharisees who opposed Jesus than the disciples who followed him?

- What is the difference between Christian legalism and a sincere attempt to live a life transformed by grace?

Topic Two: Saying Yes to Jesus

When joining the church in a few weeks, you will be asked to give your allegiance to Jesus as your Lord and Savior. On the basis of your study of today's portion of the catechism, what does this mean?

Many people find it helpful to think of joining the church as a covenant-making or covenant-renewing service. Just as you make a covenant in a marriage ceremony, so, too, do you enter into a covenant with God and the church when you join the church or transfer your membership. The Presbyterian *Book of Common Worship* calls the worship service in which new members join the Reaffirmation of the Baptismal Covenant.

- What do you think will be most helpful for you to focus on in the coming weeks leading up to this service? Are there specific actions you might take prior to this service that could represent a renewed or first-time commitment to Christ? Often, people find it helpful to share their new commitment with others. Are there friends or family with whom you would like to do so?

- Consider studying the service that will be used when the new members join the church. Invite them to ask questions about the promises they will make.

WHAT DOES THIS MEAN FOR ME TODAY?

1. Sing or read the hymns "I Greet Thee Who My Sure Redeemer Art!" (#457 in *The Presbyterian Hymnal*) or "Crown Him with Many Crowns"(#151 in *The Presbyterian Hymnal*). Ask for feelings after

singing or reading these great hymns. Has your sense or image of Jesus Christ changed because of our time together? If so, how?

2. Invite the participants to decide on one thing they will do this week as a symbolic act of their commitment to Christ. Have them write it down on a piece of paper, put it in an envelope, seal it, write their name on the front, and hand it into the leader. Tell them you will give them out next week and see if people were able to follow through on their commitments.

CLOSING

As we recite together the Apostles' Creed, think carefully about the meaning of the words. Repeat the Apostles' Creed together and close with prayer.

The Saving Significance of Jesus' Death

The *Study Catechism*: Questions 42–52

Question 42. What do you affirm when you say that he "suffered under Pontius Pilate"?

First, that our Lord was humiliated, rejected, and abused by the temporal authorities of his day, both religious and political. Christ thus aligned himself with all human beings who are oppressed, tortured, or otherwise shamefully treated by those with worldly power. Second, and even more importantly, that our Lord, though innocent, submitted himself to condemnation by an earthly judge so that through him we ourselves, though guilty, might be acquitted before our heavenly Judge.

Luke 18:32	Ps. 9:9
2 Cor. 5:21	Luke 1:52
Isa. 53:3	2 Tim. 4:8

Question 43. What do you affirm when you say that he was "crucified, dead, and buried"?

That when our Lord passed through the door of real human death, he showed us that there is no sorrow he has not known, no grief he has not borne, and no price he was unwilling to pay in order to reconcile us to God.

Matt. 26:38–39	Heb. 2:9
Isa. 53:5	2 Cor. 5:19
Gal. 3:13	

Question 44. What do you affirm when you say that he "descended into hell"?

That our Lord took upon himself the full consequences of our sinfulness, even the agony of abandonment by God, in order that we might be spared.

Mark 15:34   Rom. 4:24—25

Heb. 9:26

Question 45. Why did Jesus have to suffer as he did?

Because grace is more abundant—and sin more serious—than we suppose. However cruelly we may treat one another, all sin is primarily against God. God condemns sin, yet never judges apart from grace. In giving Jesus Christ to die for us, God took the burden of our sin into God's own self to remove it once and for all. The cross in all its severity reveals an abyss of sin swallowed up by the suffering of divine love.

Rom. 8:1, 3–4   Col. 1:20

1 Cor. 1:18   James 2:13

Rom. 5:8

Question 46. What do you affirm when you say that "on the third day he rose again from the dead"?

That our Lord could not be held by the power of death. Having died on the cross, he appeared to his followers, triumphant from the grave, in a new, exalted kind of life. In showing them his hands and his feet, the one who was crucified revealed himself to them as the Lord and Savior of the world.

Acts 2:24   John 20:15–18

1 Cor. 15:3–4   1 Cor. 15:5–8

Luke 24:36–40   John 20:27

Question 47. What do you affirm when you say that "he ascended into heaven and is seated at the right hand of the Father"?

First, that Christ has gone to be with the Father, hidden except to the eyes of faith. Second, however, that Christ is not cut off from us in the remote past, or in some place from which he cannot reach us, but is present to us here and now by grace. He reigns with divine authority, protecting us, guiding us, and interceding for us until he returns in glory.

Acts 1:6–11   Col. 3:1

Question 48. How do you understand the words that "he will come again to judge the living and the dead"?

Like everyone else, I too must stand in fear and trembling before the judgment seat of Christ. But the Judge is the one who submitted to judgment for my sake. Nothing will be able to separate me from the love of God in Christ Jesus my Lord. All the sinful failures that cause me shame will perish as through fire, while any good I may have done will be received with gladness by God.

2 Cor. 5:10   1 John 4:17

Eccl. 12:14   1 Cor. 3:12–15

Acts 17:31   Acts 10:42

Rom. 8:38–39

Question 49. Will all human beings be saved?

No one will be lost who can be saved. The limits to salvation, whatever they may be, are known only to God. Three truths above all are certain. God is a holy God who is not to be trifled with. No one will be saved except by grace alone. And no judge could possibly be more gracious than our Lord and Savior, Jesus Christ.

Heb. 10:31   John 3:17–18

Rom. 11:32   Ezek. 18:32

Eph. 2:8   2 Cor. 5:14–15

1 Tim. 2:3–4   Luke 15:4–7

Question 50. Is Christianity the only true religion?

Religion is a complex matter. When used as a means to promote self-justification, war-mongering, or prejudice, it is a form of sin. Too often all religions—and not least Christianity—have been twisted in this way. Nevertheless, by grace, despite all disobedience, Christianity offers the truth of the gospel. Although other religions may enshrine various truths, no other can or does affirm the name of Jesus Christ as the hope of the world.

Matt. 7:3	John 14:6
James 1:26	Rom. 1:16
James 1:27	2 Cor. 4:7
Acts 4:12	

Question 51. How will God deal with the followers of other religions?

God has made salvation available to all human beings through Jesus Christ, crucified and risen. How God will deal with those who do not know or follow Christ, but who follow another tradition, we cannot finally say. We can say, however, that God is gracious and merciful, and that God will not deal with people in any other way than we see in Jesus Christ, who came as the Savior of the world.

Rev. 7:9	John 3:19
Ps. 103:8	Titus 2:11

Question 52. How should I treat non-Christians and people of other religions?

As much as I can, I should meet friendship with friendship, hostility with kindness, generosity with gratitude, persecution with forbearance, truth with agreement, and error with truth. I should express my faith with humility and devotion as the occasion requires, whether silently or openly, boldly or meekly, by word or by deed. I should avoid compromising the truth on the one hand and being narrow-minded on the other. In short, I should always welcome and accept these others in a way that honors and reflects the Lord's welcome and acceptance of me.

Rom. 15:7	Luke 6:37
Matt. 5:44	Eph. 4:25
Acts. 13:47	Rom. 12:21
Rom. 13:10	

Theological Background

THE PASSION OF CHRIST

Questions 42–45 of the *Study Catechism* concern the events surrounding our Lord's execution. The story of those events can lose their power for Christians because we inevitably become so familiar with them. Dorothy L. Sayers, who wrote good theology as well as good detective fiction, has remarked, "It is curious that people who are filled with horrified indignation whenever a cat kills a sparrow can hear the story of the killing of God . . . and not experience any shock at all."[11] The *Study Catechism* does not sugarcoat the passion of Christ. The words here are aptly vivid: humiliation, torture, grief, hell, agony, death. For Easter to come, Good Friday must come first.

Pontius Pilate's presence in the creed is an odd fact that has always called for explanation. In addition to the two interpretations the *Catechism* mentions (question 42), many theologians have pointed out that Jesus' suffering "under Pontius Pilate" locates these events in a particular time and place. The human life of God in Jesus of Nazareth is not some idealistic spiritual possibility open in principle to anyone who will lead a radically God-oriented life. As we saw in question 30, Jesus Christ is unique in that, "No one else will ever be God incarnate." When we affirm in the creed that he "suffered under Pontius Pilate," we state our belief in the concrete particularity of God's unique human life as an unrepeatable event that happened once in history, having significance for all time and eternity.

"Real human death" (question 43) ends Jesus' suffering. Karl Barth was of the opinion that the creed means to punctuate the genuine humanity of Christ's death with the affirmation of his burial.[12] It is characteristically (though not universally) human to attach great significance to the burial of the dead. Christ's burial signifies that he was truly and absolutely dead.

The descent of our Lord into hell has been a problematic affirmation for many Christians. At one time it was a widespread practice for many Presbyterians to omit this affirmation from the creed. At least one official hymnal of the Presbyterian Church in this century printed the creed with a footnote here, inviting those who so desired to omit the affirmation that Christ descended into hell. To omit this article, though, is to omit the confession that the Lordship of Jesus Christ extends to every part of creation and every experience of human life. If Christ did not descend into hell, then his Lordship is limited. The power of evil has nowhere to hide from the redeeming power of God in Jesus Christ.

THE RESURRECTION AND ASCENSION OF CHRIST

Easter is the basic Christian holiday. Because of the stress we place on Christmas in our culture, it can be hard to remember that it receives all its light from Easter. Because Christ was raised from the dead, we know his birth, life, and suffering have importance that transcend his own lifetime. Easter is an event within the flow of world history, but it was not produced by the causes that produce history. Karl Barth expressed this with a mathematical analogy: Easter touches history as a tangent touches a circle, that is, at a single mathematical point. The analogy breaks down when we recognize that Easter has consequences in history long after it occurred. However it is both true and important that Easter is not a consequence or an effect of any other reality or occurrence in history. Its only cause is the act of God, defeating the power of death and evil over us.

The Easter event is not, judging by the biblical accounts, a mere resuscitation of Jesus' body. Resuscitation is what happened to Lazarus, for example, or to the little girl Tabitha. They came to life, lived a while more, then died again.

The affirmation that "He ascended into heaven and sits at the right hand of God" is easy for those who wish to be theologically sophisticated to ridicule because of the metaphors of ascension ("going up") and sitting. The idea that heaven is not "up there" is not an insight of the modern scientific mind, though. In his treatise "On the Incarnation," the great fourth-century theologian Athanasius of Alexandria already realized the need for a more sophisticated view, and suggested that heaven (by which he did not mean what we call space) surrounds the earth. As John Calvin put it, ". . . it is a question, not of the disposition of his body, but of the majesty of his authority."[13]

THE RETURN OF CHRIST AND THE WORLD'S RELIGIONS

It is difficult to imagine a more careful, nuanced, and accurate treatment of the problem of Christianity and the religions of the world than it receives in the *Study Catechism.* To deal accurately with this issue is to walk the edge of a knife. There is a risk of falling off the edge, on the one hand, into a naive universalism that depletes the energy of the gospel, and the uniqueness of Jesus Christ, by simplistically claiming that every spiritual and religious impulse and system is as valid a "path to God" as any other. On the other hand, there is a risk of falling off into the flat assertion that there is no other way to know God truly except participation in the institutional Christian church. This latter error not only seems to foreclose God's options, it appears to be a contradiction of scripture, which affirms in Romans 9–11 and elsewhere that the Jews, at least, will again be "grafted in" to God's Kingdom.

For Further Study

The works of P. T. Forsyth run deep with insight concerning the significance of Christ's passion and have recently begun to be reprinted by Wipf & Stock Publishers of Eugene, Oregon. See especially *The Work of Christ* and *The Cruciality of the Cross.*

For further study of the passion's place in the creed, including the presence of Pilate, see J. N. D. Kelly, *Early Christian Creeds* (New York: Longman, 1973).

There is no more difficult or contentious issue in contemporary theology than the relation of Christianity to the world's religions. Extremist views on either side are readily available and easily found. The most nuanced treatment of which I am aware is Lesslie Newbigin, *The Finality of Christ* (London: SCM, 1969), chapter 2: "Christianity Among the Religions."

Preparation and Materials Needed

- Read over carefully the background material and the lesson plan.
- Make decisions where necessary about optional activities, whether to divide into small groups, etc.
- Provide nametags and markers.
- Have newsprint or a wipe board available.
- Provide a VCR and monitor and a video depicting the crucifixion. (See suggestions given under "Getting Started" on page 70.) Optional.
- Provide a cassette tape player or CD player and a recording of the hymn "Were You There When They Crucified My Lord?". Optional.
- Write instructions for small groups (pages 72 and 75) on newsprint.

Lesson Plan—Session 5: The Saving Significance of Jesus' Death. Questions 42–52

WELCOME AND REVIEW

Greet everyone as they come in. Provide nametags if a large group.

Review lessons 1–4 by asking questions 1, 7, 15, and 29 from the catechism and having the class repeat the answers together:

Question 1. What is God's purpose for your life?

God wills that I should live by the grace of the Lord Jesus Christ, for the love of God, and in the communion of the Holy Spirit.

Question 7. What do you believe when you confess your faith in "God the Father Almighty"?

That God is a God of love, and that God's love is powerful beyond measure.

Question 15. What do you believe when you say that God is "Maker of heaven and earth"?

First, that God called heaven and earth, with all that is in them, into being out of nothing simply by the power of God's Word. Second, that by that same power all things are upheld and governed in perfect wisdom, according to God's eternal purpose.

Question 29. What do you believe when you confess your faith in Jesus Christ as "God's only Son"?

That Jesus Christ is a unique person who was sent to do a unique work.

Ask for questions or reflections about material studied in previous sessions.

Refer the group to the chart used last week outlining the *Study Catechism*'s treatment of the second article of the Apostles' Creed. Tell them that this week the class will focus on the saving significance of Christ's death and the theme of judgment.

GETTING STARTED

Choose one of the following opening activities:

1. Visualizing Scripture

    Have the participants close their eyes and visualize in their mind's eye the narrative you will read to them. Read Luke 22–24 with expression. Following the reading, invite the participants to gather in groups of two or three to share the part of the story that was most vivid. What stuck out? What new insights occurred as a result of this experience?

2. Watching a Video

    A video presentation on the crucifixion and resurrection also can bring this story to life. Preview the tape and have the tape set for the portion you want to show. Time will limit how much you can show.

The crucifixion and resurrection portions are the most powerful visually. Consider using "The New Media Bible—Luke" or the *Reader's Digest Video Series* "Jesus and His Times," Tape 3: "His Last Days."

3. Listening to a Recording

    Listen to a recording of "Were You There When They Crucified My Lord?" on audio tape or CD. Invite the group to reflect on the words and events. (This activity takes the shortest length of time and is good to use with a group that is familiar with the story.)

WHAT DOES THE CHURCH CONFESS?

1. Read responsively catechism questions 42–47.

2. Introduce biblical images describing the saving significance of Jesus' death.

    Consider introducing this section with comments like the following: This week we are focusing on one of the most important and difficult aspects of Christianity, the saving significance of Jesus' death. We are brought face to face with this topic in that part of the Apostles' Creed that tells us Jesus "suffered under Pontius Pilate, was crucified, dead, and buried." This is treated in questions 42–45 of the *Study Catechism*. It is important to realize that the catechism does not treat the significance of Jesus' death in isolation from the entire work by which reconciliation between God and humanity is effected. The incarnation of the Son, his earthly ministry, his death and resurrection, and his ascension are together the one act of salvation by which God overcomes the forces of sin and death separating humanity from God. Perhaps the most important theme woven throughout the entire catechism is the triumph of God's suffering love. As early as question 2 of the catechism this note is sounded. It continues to sound in other parts of the catechism as well, like question 8 in which God's power is described in terms of God's love, "a love that is ready to suffer for our sakes, yet so strong that nothing will prevail against it." The death of Jesus, thus, can be seen as the culmination of God's suffering love, which animates every aspect of his earthly ministry.

    Nonetheless, Jesus' death on the cross has been singled out by the church as having special significance in the overall work of reconciliation. The New Testament repeatedly returns to this theme in its summary statements of the gospel and uses a number of different images to describe the significance of Jesus' death.

In groups of three or four, let's look at some of the ways the New Testament describes the significance of Jesus' death. Ask each group to look up the passages listed below and discuss the following questions (write the instructions on newsprint before class to post at the front of the room):

- What is the primary image used in these passages to describe Jesus' death?
- In what life setting may this image have originated?
- Are there comparable settings in our world that allow this image to resonate with contemporary experience? If so, what are they? What might be some ways of translating this image into contemporary terms?
- Please be prepared to make a brief summary of your findings to the total group.

Do not tell the group in advance which image they are focusing on.

Group 1—Mk. 10:45; 1 Cor. 6:19, 7:23; Gal. 3:13, 4:4–5; Eph. 1:7; 1 Tim. 2:6

Group 2—Heb. 2:17, 7:27, 9:25–28; Eph. 5:2; 1 Cor. 5:7.

Group 3—Rom. 4:25; 5:6–11, 16; Gal. 2:16

Consider adding the following background information to the group's insights when it is discussed in the total group.

- *Ransom; redeem*

    Lying behind these passages is the practice of providing payment that releases a person from an obligation to which he or she is bound. In the Old Testament, if an Israelite in dire poverty sold himself into slavery, a friend or relative might "redeem" him by providing a payment (Lev. 25:51). Similarly, a ransom could be paid to free captives taken in war (Isa. 45:13). In the Greek world of the New Testament period, these terms were associated with two common settings: (1) the price paid to redeem something given as a pledge or in pawn, and (2) payment to the owner of a slave to buy freedom. In their use of this term, thus, various authors of the New Testament portray Jesus' death as a ransom paid to free humanity from slavery to sin, a condition from which humanity was utterly incapable of freeing itself.

Jesus pays the price for our freedom. He ransoms us from our captivity.

- *Sacrifice/atonement*

  The idea of atonement is quite prominent in the Old Testament and is closely related to the activities of the priest who offers a sacrifice to atone for the sins of an individual or the people as a whole. See, for example, Exodus 30:10, Leviticus 4:20, and Leviticus 5:6. Such sacrifices were thought to cleanse the people from their impurity and restore them to a proper relationship with God and those against whom they had sinned. The book of Hebrews in the New Testament draws on this image extensively, portraying Jesus as the high priest who offered himself as a once-and-for-all sacrifice to remove the sins of humanity (see Heb. 9:11–10:18). The image appears elsewhere in the New Testament, as in the passages noted above. Jesus' death atones for humanity's sins. It is the perfect sacrifice by which a sinful humanity is made clean and restored to a proper relationship to God and one another.

- *Justification/judgment*

  The language of justification and judgment comes from the legal sphere. As used in Paul, something like the following scene seems to be in mind: The scene is a courtroom. The accused stands before the judge. No doubt exists that he is guilty as charged, so guilty that the only sentence can be death. The judge, having pronounced the sentence of death, then does something that is unthinkable. He leaves his position of power and asks that the sentence be executed on him instead of the condemned person. The judge dies in the place of the guilty party, who stands acquitted by virtue of this free, unmerited, and unimaginable gift. The courtroom image is valuable in that it brings out the true guilt of the accused, the deserved sentence of death, and the unexpected turn whereby the guilty is acquitted because the judge elects to die in the guilty party's stead.

Alternatively, you might give each group some study resources providing this information, allowing them to integrate it into their presentation to the total group. In making their presentations, each group should take no more than five minutes to present their findings.

Following their presentations, point out to the groups that these various ways of understanding Jesus' death are complementary. They all appear at some point in the *Study Catechism*. The image of ransom/redemption appears in answer 2; atonement/ sacrifice appears in answer 40.

In its treatment of Jesus' suffering at the hands of Pontius Pilate, the *Study Catechism* draws on the justification/judgment image. This is to be expected because of the legal nature of Jesus' appearance before Pilate. As the catechism points out, Jesus' condemnation at the hands of an earthly judge represents far more than a simple legal proceeding. Here, Jesus receives the death sentence rightly falling on a sinful humanity. The Son of God, with the power and authority to judge humanity, takes this judgment on himself thereby acquitting (or justifying in Paul's language) humanity before God. The judge is judged in our place.

WHAT DO I THINK?

Once we have grasped this important biblical understanding of the saving significance of Jesus' death, we are compelled to think about the judgment of God in a new way. This is the topic for reflection in today's session. The *Study Catechism* leads us directly to this topic in its explication of the Apostles' Creed's statement: "he will come to judge the living and the dead."

1. Invite the group to begin this part of the session by sharing in pairs some of the images of judgment they have encountered over the course of their lives. Then ask for quick sharing in the total group.

2. Direct the group's attention to answer 48 and ask them to read it responsively. Lead a brief discussion of the answer with questions like the following:

   - **Why does the answer begin by reminding all of us that we will stand "in fear and trembling before the judgment seat of Christ"?** (Perhaps it wants to make sure that we do not begin by focusing on God's judgment toward others, reminding each and every one of us that the sentence of guilt falls on us too.)

   - The catechism, then, creates a link with answer 42, which we have just been studying. **What is that link? Why is it important for each one of us to remember that the One who will judge us is the One who was judged in our place?**

   - The very love of God, ready to suffer for our sakes, is too strong a bond to be broken. In the concluding sentence of this answer, the *Study Catechism* invites us to consider our good and bad deeds in light of the love revealed in Christ. **What sorts of attitudes might this way of thinking about God's judgment elicit? How do they compare with other attitudes accompanying some of the images of judgment shared at the beginning of this part of the session?**

3. The *Study Catechism* invites us to draw on this understanding of God's judgment to reflect, not only on our own lives, but God's treatment of the members of other religions and those outside the faith. The questions and answers found in 49–52 are some of the most interesting and challenging of the entire catechism. Some of the answers are "ponderables": answers that are not straightforward but are designed to invite thinking and discussion. They can be returned to again and again over the course of a person's life.

   Divide the class into four groups. Direct class members to *Study Catechism* questions 49–52 and the accompanying scripture passages, found in the *Student Guide* on pages 47–49. Assign each group one of the questions from this section. Ask them to begin by reading the question silently several times and then discussing it using the following questions, written on newsprint:

   • What are the basic points covered in the answer?

   • In light of the scripture references, does the answer seem to be grounded in the Bible? If so, why? If not, why?

   • If we consider this answer in light of what we've just studied about Jesus' death—the judge judged in our place—what does this add to our reflections?

   • What are some of the most important implications of this answer for our attitude toward others?

   • If the catechism teaches us what Presbyterians believe about God's judgment—toward ourselves and those outside the faith—how does this differ from the way judgment is portrayed by other branches of Christianity? Do you find its teaching challenging, reassuring, unsettling, or something with which you disagree? Discuss why you feel this way.

WHAT DOES THIS MEAN FOR ME TODAY?

The final part of the session might be conducted using one of the following activities:

1. Guided meditation

   Call the four groups together and tell them that you will begin the next session by asking for the insights gained from their small group discussion. Tell them that during the final part of your time together you are going to ask them to enter a meditative, prayerful state in which they visualize themselves and their loved ones basking in the light of God's love. Invite the participants to close their eyes and focus on their breathing, relaxing their various muscle groups one at a time.

   In a soft voice, paint a vivid word picture in which the participants visualize themselves in Jesus' presence. Help them focus on feelings of warmth and acceptance that radiate from Jesus. What would they like to share with him? How can this wise and gracious judge grant them a new perspective on issues troubling them? Are there other family members whom they would like to join them in Jesus' presence? Invite them to do so and to continue the conversation. End by asking the participants to gently bring themselves back into the present, opening their eyes.

2. Judging Ourselves and Others

   Invite the four groups to come back together. Do not ask for reports from each group. Instead, invite individuals to share briefly the most important insights emerging from their group's discussion of judgment. Invite them to reflect silently on one person or situation that consistently elicits a judgmental attitude on their part. Perhaps they are too judgmental toward themselves, their children, an ex-spouse, or a coworker. How might they reframe this in light of what they have learned during this class meeting? What concrete steps would be most helpful in giving up their judgmental attitude and learning to view others with the same loving spirit that Christ holds toward them? If the group members feel comfortable sharing with one another, invite them to pair off and share. Otherwise, end the time of silent reflection by offering a prayer in which the participants are asked to silently pray that God might help them learn to judge themselves and others as God does.

CLOSING

Invite the group to end the class by saying together the Apostles' Creed.

Who Is the Holy Spirit?

The *Study Catechism:* Questions 53–61

Question 53. What is the third article of the Apostles' Creed?

"I believe in the Holy Spirit, the holy catholic church, the communion of saints, the forgiveness of sins, the resurrection of the body, and the life everlasting. Amen."

Question 54. What do you believe when you confess your faith in the Holy Spirit?

Apart from the Holy Spirit, our Lord can neither be loved, nor known, nor served. The Holy Spirit is the personal bond by which Jesus Christ unites us to himself, the teacher who opens our hearts to Christ, and the comforter who leads us to repentance, empowering us to live in Christ's service. As the work of the one Holy Spirit, our love, knowledge, and service of Christ are all inseparably related.

John 14:26	1 Cor. 12:3
Rom. 5:5	1 Cor. 6:17, 19
1 Cor. 3:16	John 4:24

Question 55. How do we receive the Holy Spirit?

By receiving the Word of God. As the midwife of the new creation, the Spirit arrives with the Word, brings us to rebirth, and assures us of eternal life. The Spirit nurtures, corrects, and strengthens us with the pure spiritual milk of the Word (1 Peter 2:2).

Eph. 6:17	John 14:16–17

John 3:5–6   Luke 11:13

1 Thess. 1:5   John 16:8

Rom. 8:15–16   1 Pet. 2:2

Question 56. What do you mean when you speak of "the Word of God"?

"Jesus Christ as he is attested for us in Holy Scripture is the one Word of God whom we have to hear, and whom we have to trust and obey in life and in death" (Barmen Declaration, Article I).

John 1:1–5   John 1:14

Question 57. Isn't Holy Scripture also the Word of God?

Yes. Holy Scripture is also God's Word because of its content, its function, and its origin. Its central content is Jesus Christ, the living Word. Its basic function is to deepen our love, knowledge, and service of him as our Savior and Lord. And its ultimate origin is in the Holy Spirit, who spoke through the prophets and apostles, and who inspires us with eager desire for the truths that scripture contains.

2 Tim. 3:16   John 5:39

Question 58. Isn't preaching also the Word of God?

Yes. Preaching and other forms of Christian witness are also God's Word when they are faithful to the witness of Holy Scripture. By the power of the Spirit, preaching actually gives to us what it proclaims—the real presence of our Lord Jesus Christ. Faith comes by hearing God's Word in the form of faithful proclamation.

Mark 16:15   Rom. 1:15–16

2 Cor. 4:5   Rom. 10:17

Question 59. Does the Holy Spirit ever speak apart from God's Word in its written and proclaimed forms?

Since the Spirit is not given to the church without the Word, true proclamation depends on Scripture. Since the Word cannot be grasped without the Spirit, true interpretation depends on prayer. However, as the wind blows where it will, so may the Spirit speak or work in people's lives in unexpected or indirect ways, yet always according to the Word, never contradicting or diluting it.

John 3:8   2 Pet. 1:20–21

Acts 8:29–31   Eph. 6:18

Question 60. Aren't people without faith sometimes wiser than those who have faith?

Yes. The important question for the church is not so much where an insight may come from as the norm by which to test it. Truth is where one finds it, whether inside or outside the church, and whether supporting or contradicting one's own most cherished opinions. Our faithful discernment of what is true, however, depends finally on God's Word as conveyed in Holy Scripture. The church is therefore reformed and always being reformed according to the Word of God.

Titus 1:9   Isa. 45:4

Luke 16:8b   Num. 22:28

Question 61. Doesn't modern critical scholarship undermine your belief that Holy Scripture is a form of God's Word?

No. The methods of modern scholarship are a good servant but a bad master. They are neither to be accepted nor rejected uncritically. Properly used they help us rightly and richly interpret Scripture; improperly used they can usurp the place of faith (or establish an alternative faith). Wise interpreters use these methods in the service of faithful witness and understanding. The methods of modern scholarship remain a useful tool, while Holy Scripture remains reliable in all essential matters of faith and practice.

Prov. 1:5–6   1 Cor. 1:20, 25

Prov. 10:14

Theological Background

The Holy Spirit, according to the Reformed tradition of Christian theology, is always experienced in connection with the Word of God in its threefold form: incarnate in Jesus Christ, written in scripture, and preached in the church. As the *Study Catechism* puts it, we receive the Holy Spirit, "By receiving the Word of God" (question 55). Jesus Christ is the first "form" of the Word of God. He is the Word of God that has become flesh, in the language of the Gospel of John. The Holy Spirit is therefore the Spirit of Christ.

THE WORD OF GOD WRITTEN

The Word of God in its written form is the central form of the Word of God. The first form is the incarnation of God in Jesus Christ, yet we have access to this only through the Word of God written. On the other hand is the Word of God preached, yet the Word of God is preached only when the Word written is interpreted under the guidance of the Holy Spirit.

Most basically, the association of the Holy Spirit with the Word of God means we receive the Spirit as God's illumination in reading the Word of God written in the biblical witness of the prophets and apostles to Jesus Christ. As has often been observed, the reader of scripture is as inspired as the scripture itself. As John Calvin put it, "the Word is the instrument by which the Lord dispenses the illumination of his Spirit to believers. For they know no other Spirit than him who spoke and dwelt in the apostles. . . ."[14]

From the beginning, Christians in the Reformed tradition have affirmed that scripture alone, interpreted with the light of the Holy Spirit who lives in the lives of Christ's adopted brothers and sisters, is the reliable rule of our faith and morals. It is this principle, the principle of *sola Scriptura*, scripture alone, that is expressed in questions 59 and 60 of the *Study Catechism*. Whereas it is true, as a great advocate of the *sola Scriptura* principle picturesquely conceded, that "God may speak to us through Russian Communism, a flute concerto, a blossoming shrub, or a dead dog,"[15] it is also the case, as the catechism puts it, that "our faithful discernment of what is true . . . depends finally on God's word as conveyed in Holy Scripture. The church is therefore reformed and always being reformed according to the Word of God."

To be a church reformed and always being reformed is to be a church that continually measures its preaching, teaching, and forms of life against the standard of scripture as the Word of God written, which is the unique and authoritative witness to the incarnation of God in Jesus Christ. It is a very common error to say that "reformed and always being reformed" means we are constantly changing things to keep up to date. In fact it means we must constantly allow God to correct us and purify us through the biblical witness. The gains of the Reformation are never secure against our human tendency to make gods for ourselves. We must return to scripture again and again to find the resources to purify our life together as the Body of Christ, and thus be in the truest sense a Reformed church.

The catechism uses a proverb that goes back at least to the eighteenth century in America to describe the place of modern biblical scholarship in our believing efforts to understand the Bible as scripture. Applying this proverb, we learn that such methods are like fire in a house: "A good servant but a bad master." In other words, strategies for interpreting scripture are useful to the church and to the life of faith as far as they help us understand the biblical text itself. However, every mature Christian has seen interpretative methods turned against the text in a way that erroneously corrodes faith. Very often in the last century and a half, such methods have been based on the questionable assumption of historicism, the idea that the meaning of history is to be found within history itself. Christians understand that the meaning of history is to be found in God's purposes and acts, which are never limited by history. Our reading of the biblical witness to God's acts must therefore be illuminated but not limited—served but not mastered—by historical insight. The historicist error most often comes out in commentaries and sermons that interpret some hypothetical circumstance outside the text or the history of the text's composition, rather than interpreting what the words themselves say.

THE WORD OF GOD PREACHED

Preaching in the church extends into our time and place the witness of the prophets and apostles. This is the sense in which preaching is also the Word of God.

The church's conviction that preaching is a form of the Word of God does not claim the authority of God for what is preached no matter what. This reality depends first of all on the action of God, bearing witness through the Holy Spirit to Jesus Christ. It also depends upon the preacher's commitment to interpret and apply the biblical witness. Preaching that is determined to continue the witness of the prophets and apostles into our age can be, by God's grace, the Word of God. However, that claim would not be valid for preaching which attacks that witness or which relativizes it by placing the preacher's own opinions alongside it as an alternative.

For Further Study

For Calvin's doctrine of scripture, see his *Institutes of the Christian Religion*, 1.6–9 (Philadelphia: Westminster Press, 1960). The chapter on the Reformers in Karl Barth's little tract, "No! An Answer to Emil Brunner," though published in a context of serious theological conflict, leaves little to be desired as a short summary of Calvin's teaching on this point. This was published in English in the volume *Nature and Grace,* John Baillie, ed. (London: Geoffrey Bles: The Centenary Press, 1946).

For a classic exposition of the threefold form of the Word of God, see Karl Barth, *Church Dogmatics,* G. W. Bromiley and T. F. Torrance eds. (Edinburgh: T. & T. Clark, 1975), 1:88–124.

Preparation and Materials Needed

- Read over carefully the background material and the lesson plan.
- Make decisions where necessary about optional activities, whether to divide into small groups, etc.
- Provide nametags and markers.
- Make a copy of the Modern Critical Scholarship Spectrum on page 90 and post it at the front of the room. Provide red and green markers or stickers for this exercise.
- Write out on newsprint or make copies of the instructions for small groups on pages 86 and 87.
- Have newsprint or a wipe board available.
- Write the outline of the third article of the Apostles' Creed (page 85) on newsprint.

Lesson Plan—Session 6: Who Is the Holy Spirit? Questions 53–61

WELCOME AND REVIEW

Greet everyone as they come in. Provide nametags if a large group.

Review lessons 1–5 by asking questions 1, 7, 15, 29, and 45 from the catechism and having the class repeat the answers together:

> *Question 1. What is God's purpose for your life?*
>
> God wills that I should live by the grace of the Lord Jesus Christ, for the love of God, and in the communion of the Holy Spirit.

Question 7. What do you believe when you confess your faith in "God the Father Almighty"?

That God is a God of love, and that God's love is powerful beyond measure.

Question 15. What do you believe when you say that God is "Maker of heaven and earth"?

First, that God called heaven and earth, with all that is in them, into being out of nothing simply by the power of God's Word. Second, that by that same power all things are upheld and governed in perfect wisdom, according to God's eternal purpose.

Question 29. What do you believe when you confess your faith in Jesus Christ as "God's only Son"?

That Jesus Christ is a unique person who was sent to do a unique work.

Question 45. Why did Jesus have to suffer as he did?

Because grace is more abundant—and sin more serious—than we suppose. However cruelly we may treat one another, all sin is primarily against God. God condemns sin, yet never judges apart from grace. In giving Jesus Christ to die for us, God took the burden of our sin into God's own self to remove it once and for all. The cross in all its severity reveals an abyss of sin swallowed up by the suffering of divine love.

Ask for questions or reflections about material studied in previous sessions.

GETTING STARTED

Choose one of the following opening activities.

1. A Guided Meditation on the Holy Spirit in Our Lives

    Lead the group through the following exercise of remembering. Invite them to close their eyes if they wish, or to jot notes in their journals.

    Remember a time when you were led to do something kind you would not normally do, perhaps a time when you surprised even yourself with your compassion.

(Pause for one minute)

Remember a time when a worship service had a special impact on you, or when a sermon or Bible study seemed to be speaking directly to you.

(Pause for one minute)

Remember a time when somehow you were comforted in the midst of pain or trouble. Perhaps someone offered you a word of encouragement, or you saw one ray of hope in the midst of despair.

(Pause for one minute)

Now, open your eyes (or stop writing) and in groups of two or three, share one of the things you remembered.

These stories are evidence of the Holy Spirit in our midst. The Holy Spirit inspires us to live a new life together in love. The Holy Spirit enables us to hear and accept the gospel. The Holy Spirit gives us comfort. We don't see the Holy Spirit acting in our lives all the time, but God's presence through the Holy Spirit is always powerfully there.

2. The Story of Pentecost

Invite a gifted storyteller from your congregation to prepare and present the story of Pentecost as found in Acts 2. They might consider telling the story from the perspective of Peter, or perhaps a woman or man in the crowd, and dressing accordingly. Following the presentation, invite class members in groups of two or three to reflect on the following questions:

- What changes in attitude and demeanor do you expect took place in the disciples following Pentecost? What might have been some of their emotions between Christ's ascension and Pentecost, and how might these have changed following Pentecost?

- Which character in the story do you most closely identify with? Peter? One of the disciples? A receptive member of the crowd? A stranger from out of town? One of those who initially mocked the bizarre behavior of the disciples?

WHAT DOES THE CHURCH CONFESS?

1. An Overview of the Third Article as Treated in the *Study Catechism*.

Provide the participants with a brief overview to the *Study Catechism*'s treatment of the third article of the Apostles' Creed. By and large, it covers topics as they appear in the creed, expanding different themes at points. Consider writing the following on poster paper or newsprint.

The Third Article of the Apostles' Creed	Question 53
The Holy Spirit	54–61
Who Is the Holy Spirit and How Do We Receive It?	54–55
The Word of God: Jesus Christ, Holy Scripture, Preaching	56–61
The Holy Catholic Church	62–65
The Mission of the Church	63–65
Communion of Saints	66–67
Sacraments	68–79
Baptism	71–76
Trinity	75–76
Lord's Supper	77–79
Forgiveness of Sins	80–83
Resurrection of the Body; Christian Hope	84–86
Life Everlasting	87–88

2. Read *Study Catechism* questions 53–55 responsively. Have one person read the questions and the rest of the group respond with the answers. Direct class members to page 55 in the *Student Guide.*

3. Who is the Holy Spirit?

(Consider writing the scripture passages and questions on newsprint before class and posting them at the front of the room at this time.)

Divide into groups of three or four. Ask each group to focus on question 54 and look up the following scripture passages:

John 14:26   1 Corinthians 3:16

Romans 5:5   1 Corinthians 16:17, 19

1 Corinthians 12:3

Use these scripture passages and question 54 to answer the following three questions. (If you have three or more groups, assign one question to each group. If you have two or fewer groups, let each group work through all three questions.)

Who/What is the Holy Spirit? (List names and roles)

What does the Spirit do? (List functions)

How are we connected to the Holy Spirit? What is our relationship?

After the groups have had a chance to work through their questions, bring the class back together. Go through the three questions one at a time and invite groups to share their findings. List the responses on the wipe board or newsprint under the question headings.

4. Draw class members' attention to question 55.

   Ask, **What are some of the roles and functions of a midwife? Has anyone here witnessed a birth attended by a midwife?**

   How does the Holy Spirit serve as a midwife?

   Ask for volunteers to look up and read Luke 11:13, Romans 8:15–16, and 1 Thessalonians 1:5. Ask, **Do any of these scripture passages prompt new insights or questions?**

5. Invite the class to read catechism questions and answers 56–61 responsively. See page 56 in the *Student Guide.*

6. "The Word of God is Jesus Christ. Holy Scripture is also the Word of God. Preaching is also the Word of God." Let's take a closer look at what this means.

   Divide into three groups. (If you have fewer than six participants, do this activity as one group. If you have a very large class, divide into more than three groups and assign some or all of the questions to more than one group. Write the instructions out on newsprint before class, or make copies of this section for each group.)

   Group 1: The Word of God is Jesus Christ.

   Look at question 56 and look up John 1:1–4 and John 1:14.

   What does it mean that Jesus Christ is the "Word of God"?

   We do not live in the time of Jesus. How do we know him and thus the Word of God?

   How are we to respond to Jesus as the Word of God?

   Group 2: The Word of God is also the Holy Scripture.

   Look at question 57 and look up 2 Timothy 3:16 and John 5:39.

   How is scripture related to Jesus Christ?

How does scripture function in our lives?

How is scripture related to the Holy Spirit?

Group 3: The Word of God is also preaching.

Look at question 58 and look up 2 Corinthians 4:5, Romans 1:15–16, and Romans 10:17.

How is preaching also the Word of God?

Is all preaching the Word of God, or are conditions given?

How is preaching related to the Holy Spirit?

Bring the groups back together and invite a spokesperson from each group to briefly share their findings.

What Do I Think?

(If your group is larger than twelve, you might consider breaking up into smaller groups of five or six for this portion of the discussion.)

1. Invite the group to share any questions or comments they have about the questions and answers. **Is there a phrase you particularly like? Is there a sentence or concept that is unclear or that you disagree with? If you could choose one phrase to hang on to—what would it be and why?**

2. Look together at question 60.

   Has anyone here ever found truth outside of the church or learned more of God's grace through someone who was not a Christian? Is anyone willing to briefly share such a story?

   Cherished opinions are difficult to let go of, and it is easy to look for evidence of whatever it is we want to believe. How do we know truth when we find it? How do we "test" both new truths that come our way and those traditions that we hold dear?

   Ask someone to read the final sentence of question 60 out loud. Point out that while as Presbyterians our faith and tradition is "reformed and always being reformed," such reformation is always "according to the Word of God" rather than according to the popular culture of the day or according to the religious establishment.

3. Before class, reproduce the "Modern Critical Scholarship Spectrum." If possible, blow it up to a larger size. Post this now at the front of the room. Provide a few red and green markers or small colored stickers. Invite participants to put a green mark where they

think most people in their community fall on this issue and a red mark where they think most church members fall on this issue.

Ask, **Is it possible to negotiate a middle ground between these two extremes without having an "everything is relative" approach?**

How does the proverb "a good servant but a bad master" help us to understand the role of modern critical scholarship?

What does it mean for scripture to be "reliable in all essential matters of faith and practice?"

WHAT DOES THIS MEAN FOR ME TODAY?

1. Invite the participants to discuss the following scenario and questions in groups of three or four.

   Your ninth-grade daughter comes home from school one day with an article handed out by her teacher on the Jesus Seminar (a group of scholars who assert that most of the material in the gospels did not really happen and that Jesus said very little that is attributed to him). **What are some of the questions you think she might have? How might you use the catechism questions and scripture passages as tools to explain to her how we view scripture?**

2. Invite participants to respond to the following question by writing in their journals. **Have you ever experienced a time when you have been "inspired with eager desire for the truths that scripture contains?"**
   Invite anyone who wishes to share their response with the group.

   Ask, **What are some of the roadblocks we experience when it comes to regular reading and study of scripture?**
   List responses on the wipe board or newsprint.

   Ask, **What are some of the benefits of reading and studying scripture?**
   List responses on the wipe board or newsprint.

   Ask, **Would anyone be willing to share an approach to personal Bible study that worked for them or helpful tools and resources for personal Bible study?**

   You might want to have some samples of simple Bible study or devotional guides on hand for class members to look at.

   Invite class members to take a few minutes to write in their journals any new ideas or commitments for studying scripture they have.

3. Ask, **What are some of the major decisions you have faced in life?** Write some of the responses on the wipe board in simplified form (e.g., marriage, college, job, family).

   Ask, **Did you always have a clear sense of God's leading in this decision? Of the Holy Spirit working in your life and giving you direction?**

   Ask, **How do we stay open to the leading of the Spirit?**

   You might want to mention the spiritual practice of discernment in this discussion. A good source for your own background or for class members who are interested is Frank Rogers Jr.'s chapter "Discernment," in Practicing Our Faith, Dorothy C. Bass, ed. [San Francisco: Jossey-Bass, 1998].

   Ask, **What are some of the things that get in the way of the Spirit's leading in our lives? How do we sometimes confuse our own desires with God's leading?**

   Ask, **What are some ways that we can know whether or not a leading is from God? Look at catechism questions 59 and 60 to get you started.**

CLOSING

Sing "Open My Eyes that I May See" (Hymn #324 in *The Presbyterian Hymnal*) as your closing prayer.

Modern Critical Scholarship Spectrum

Put a green mark where you think most people in your community fall on this issue and a red mark where you think most church members fall on this issue.

1   2   3   4   5   6   7   8   9   10

MCS is wrong and seeks only to destroy faith. The Bible is inerrant and was dictated by God. Everything in it is not only true but historical fact.

MCS provides the final word. If academics "prove" that Christ did not say certain things contained in the gospels, then we should take their word for it. If archaeologists demonstrate that the walls of Jericho did not exist at the time of Joshua's conquest of the promised land, then we can discard the entire Old Testament as myth and folk tale.

SESSION 7

The Church and the Sacraments

The *Study Catechism*: Questions 62–79

Question 62. What do you affirm when you speak of "the holy catholic church"?

The church is the company of all faithful people who have given their lives to Jesus Christ, as he has given and gives himself to them. Since Christ cannot be separated from his people, the church is holy because he is holy, and universal (or "catholic") in significance because he is universal in significance. Despite all its remaining imperfections here and now, the church is called to become ever more holy and catholic, for that is what it already is in Christ.

Gal. 2:20	1 Cor. 1:2
Lev. 11:44	1 Pet. 1:15–16
Rev. 5:9	

Question 63. What is the mission of the church?

The mission of the church is to bear witness to God's love for the world in Jesus Christ.

Acts 1:8	John 15:26–27
Eph. 3:8–10	

Question 64. What forms does this mission take?

The forms are as various as the forms of God's love, yet the center is always Jesus Christ. The church is faithful to its mission when it extends mercy and forgiveness to the needy in ways that point finally to him. For in the end it is always by Christ's mercy that the needs of the needy are met.

Luke 10:37   Eph. 4:32

Deut. 15:11   Acts 4:34

Question 65. Who are the needy?

The hungry need bread, the homeless need a roof, the oppressed need justice, and the lonely need fellowship. At the same time—on another and deeper level—the hopeless need hope, sinners need forgiveness, and the world needs the gospel. On this level no one is excluded, and all the needy are one. Our mission as the church is to bring hope to a desperate world by declaring God's undying love—as one beggar tells another where to find bread.

Ps. 10:12   Matt. 25:37–40

Jer. 9:23   1 Cor. 9:16

Eph. 6:19

Question 66. What do you affirm when you speak of "the communion of saints"?

All those who live in union with Christ, whether on earth or with God in heaven, are "saints." Our communion with Christ makes us members one of another. As by his death he removed our separation from God, so by his Spirit he removes all that divides us from each other. Breaking down every wall of hostility, he makes us, who are many, one body in himself. The ties that bind us in Christ are deeper than any other human relationship.

Eph. 2:19–20   Eph. 2:14

1 Cor. 12:27   Gal. 3:28

Rom. 12:5   Eph. 4:4

1 Cor. 12:4–7, 12–13

Question 67. How do you enter into communion with Christ and so with one another?

By the power of the Holy Spirit as it works through Word and Sacrament. Because the Spirit uses them for our salvation, Word and Sacrament are called "means of grace." The Scriptures acknowledge two sacraments as instituted by our Lord Jesus Christ—baptism and the Lord's Supper.

1 Cor. 10:17   1 Cor. 12:13

Col. 3:16

Question 68. What is a sacrament?

A sacrament is a special act of Christian worship, instituted by Christ, which uses a visible sign to proclaim the promise of the gospel for the forgiveness of sins and eternal life. The sacramental sign seals this promise to believers by grace and brings to them what is promised. In baptism the sign is that of water; in the Lord's Supper, that of bread and wine.

Mark 1:9–11   Mark 14:22–25

Question 69. How do you understand the relationship between the word of promise and the sacramental sign?

Take away the word of promise, and the water is merely water, or the bread and wine, merely bread and wine. But add water, or bread and wine, to the word of promise, and it becomes a visible word. In this form it does what by grace the word always does: it brings the salvation it promises, and conveys to faith the real presence of our Lord Jesus Christ. The sacraments are visible words which uniquely assure and confirm that no matter how greatly I may have sinned, Christ died also for me, and comes to live in me and with me.

Luke 24:30–31   1 Cor. 10:16

Matt. 28:20   Col. 1:27

Question 70. What is the main difference between baptism and the Lord's Supper?

While I receive baptism only once, I receive the Lord's Supper again and again. Being unrepeatable, baptism indicates not only that Christ died for our sins once and for all, but that by grace we are also united with him once and for all through faith. Being repeatable, the Lord's Supper indicates that as we turn unfilled to him again and again, our Lord continually meets us in the power of the Holy Spirit to renew and deepen our faith.

Acts 2:41   John 6:33

John 6:51   John 6:56

1 Cor. 11:26

Question 71. What is baptism?

Baptism is the sign and seal through which we are joined to Christ.

Rom. 6:3–4   Gal. 3:27

Rom. 4:11

Question 72. What does it mean to be baptized?

My baptism means that I am joined to Jesus Christ forever. I am baptized into his death and resurrection, along with all who have received him by faith. As I am baptized with water, he baptizes me with his Spirit, washing away all my sins and freeing me from their control. My baptism is a sign that one day I will rise with him in glory, and may walk with him even now in newness of life.

Col. 2:12   Mark 1:8

1 Cor. 6:11   Eph. 4:4–6

Question 73. Are infants also to be baptized?

Yes. Along with their believing parents, they are included in the great hope of the gospel and belong to the people of God. Forgiveness and faith are both promised to them as gifts through Christ's covenant with his people. These children are therefore to be received into the community by baptism, nurtured in the Word of God, and confirmed at an appropriate time by their own profession of faith.

Gen. 17:7   Acts 2:38–39

Acts 16:15   Acts 16:33

Acts 18:8

Question 74. Should infants be baptized if their parents or guardians have no relation to the church?

No. It would be irresponsible to baptize an infant without at least one Christian parent or guardian who promises to nurture the infant in the life of the community and to instruct it in the Christian faith.

Eph. 6:4   1 Cor. 7:14

2 Tim. 1:5

Question 75. In what name are you baptized?

In the name of the Trinity. After he was raised from the dead, our Lord appeared to his disciples and said to them, "Go and make disciples of all nations, baptizing them in the name of the Father and of the Son and of the Holy Spirit" (Matt. 28:19).

Matt. 28:16–20   Matt. 3:16–17

1 Pet. 1:2   1 Cor. 12:4–6

Question 76. What is the meaning of this name?

It is the name of the Holy Trinity. The Father is God, the Son is God, and the Holy Spirit is God. And yet they are not three gods, but one God in three persons. We worship God in this mystery.

2 Cor. 13:13   John 1:1–4

Rom. 8:11   John 16:13–14

John 16:15

Question 77. What is the Lord's Supper?

The Lord's Supper is the sign and seal by which our communion with Christ is renewed.

1 Cor. 10:16

Question 78. What does it mean to share in the Lord's Supper?

When we celebrate the Lord's Supper, the Lord Jesus Christ is truly present, pouring out his Spirit upon us. By his Spirit, the bread that we break and the cup that we bless share in our Lord's own body and blood. Through them he once offered our life to God; through them he now offers his life to us. As I receive the bread and the cup, remembering that Christ died even for me, I feed on him in my heart by faith with thanksgiving, and enter his risen life, so that his life becomes mine, and my life becomes his, to all eternity.

1 Cor. 11:23–26   Mark 14:22–25

Question 79. Who may receive the Lord's Supper?

All baptized Christians who rejoice in so great a gift, who confess their sins, and who draw near with faith intending to lead a new life, may receive the Lord's Supper. This includes baptized children who have expressed a desire to participate

and who have been instructed in the meaning of the sacrament
in a way they can understand.

Luke 13:29   Phil. 4:4

1 Cor. 11:28

Theological Background

THE HOLINESS AND CATHOLICITY OF THE CHURCH

The Apostles' Creed speaks of the church of Jesus Christ as "holy"
and "catholic," and the *Study Catechism* rightly interprets these affirmations in relation to Jesus Christ. The church of Jesus Christ is holy because Christ himself, to whom we are united by the Holy Spirit, is holy.
A person, place, object, or event that is said in scripture to be holy is set
aside for God. Ultimately God alone is holy, and other realities share
God's holiness when God sets them aside for sacred use. For example,
the ground around the burning bush was said to be holy, and Moses was
commanded to acknowledge this by removing his shoes. But surely
Moses had been to that place many times during his forty years keeping
Jethro's sheep! It was not that the ground itself was holy, but that on that
occasion God set it aside for a world-transforming communication with
Moses. The ground shared God's holiness while God used it. Likewise
the church is holy not in and for itself, but because it is set aside through
union with Christ for God's purposes. The undeniable fact of hypocrisy
and sin in the church therefore is not a reason for doubting its holiness.
The holiness of the church is the holiness of Christ.

The catholicity of the church is likewise not its own, but Christ's. This
teaching of the creed has to do with the universality of the church. There
is no era, no culture, no nation, and no person for whom the gospel of
Jesus Christ cannot be meaningful in an appropriate way. There is no one
in any time or place who cannot belong to the universal fellowship of
those who are spiritually united to Christ. Here again, the universality of
the church is not an achievement in which the church can take pride. It is
based on our participation in Christ, who is a universal Savior.

The catholicity of the church means that ultimately there is only
one church of Christ. As the *Book of Order* of the Presbyterian Church
(U.S.A.) acknowledges (G-4.0102), the division of the church into congregations is a matter of practical convenience and does not count
against the inner unity of the universal church. Christ is not divided!
(1 Cor. 1:13).

Augustine of Hippo defined a sacrament as "a visible form of an invisible grace,"[16] a definition John Calvin found helpful. To John Calvin, the two sacraments of baptism and the Lord's Supper were object lessons in the gospel. The philosopher Ludwig Wittgenstein taught that anything which can be said, can be said clearly; but some things cannot be said, they can only be shown." This thought accurately reflects the place of the sacraments in relation to preaching in the Reformed tradition. The Reformed have always taught that the sacraments ought never be celebrated without the preaching of a sermon that lays out clearly the claim of Christ on the hearer's lives. However, the full depth of that claim, and the sense of Christ's spiritually real presence, is best shown rather than said. As the catechism puts it, a sacrament "uses a visible sign to proclaim the promise of the gospel for the forgiveness of sins and eternal life" (question 68).

Christian baptism uses water as the physical and visible sign of the spiritual reality of our cleansing by the Holy Spirit. "As I am baptized with water, he [Christ] baptizes me with his Spirit, washing away all my sins and freeing me from their control (question 72). We baptize infants who are born into the community of those who belong to Christ, not to make them members of that community, but to acknowledge the prior act of God, who has thought of them before there was a universe, and brought them into existence within that community. There is, therefore, no reason to baptize children without at least one Christian parent or guardian who promises to nurture the infant in the life of the community and instruct it in the Christian faith (question 74). To baptize them would be irresponsible; to leave them unbaptized for the time being has no disadvantages, since they can be baptized on their own profession of faith later.

Baptism into Christ is performed in the name of the Father, Son, and Holy Spirit (questions 75, 76). This is God's identity. It is also the name in which the biblical witness to Christ teaches us to baptize (Matt. 28:19). Father, Son, and Holy Spirit is the name of the one God whom we worship: the unbegotten Father begets the Son, the Son glorifies the Father, and the two together send the Holy Spirit who is the loving Spirit of their relationship; this is the one God. Although alternatives have been proposed, there are no substitutes for naming God in this way, or for baptizing in this name. In particular, "Creator, Redeemer, Sustainer," which is sometimes given as a possible substitute, is nothing more than a partial list of things God does. It is not God's identity. "We worship God in this mystery," says the *Catechism*. It is important to notice that it is God the Trinity that is mysterious. The church's *doctrine* of the Trinity is not mysterious, only difficult.

In the Lord's Supper, the bread and cup are the physical and visible signs we use to signify the spiritual presence of Christ's body and blood. Christ's presence in the Lord's Supper is, in Calvin's way of putting it, "spiritually real." Christ's presence in the Supper is not physical or bodily in any sense, except the secondary and derivative sense in which the church is the Body of Christ through the spiritual union of believers with him. To say Christ's own physical body is present in the elements is to deny, as Calvin and many others have pointed out, the true humanity of Christ. However, we do know that Christ is spiritually present in the room as our host at the meal when it is being celebrated. This reality, though, is easier to experience than to define.

For Further Study

To learn more about what the creed means by the holiness and catholicity of the church, see J. N. D. Kelly, *Early Christian Creeds* (New York: Longman, 1973).

An excellent study of Calvin's treatment of the Lord's Supper in the larger context of Calvin's theology is Brian Gerrish's book *Grace and Gratitude* (Philadelphia: Fortress Press, 1973).

There has been a revival of interest in the doctrine of the Trinity in recent years, so there are many books of diverse quality available. Thomas F. Torrance's *The Trinitarian Faith* (Edinburgh: T. & T. Clark, 1993) is magisterial in scope and insight. One of the most accessible summaries is chapter 4 of Arthur C. McGill's small book, *Suffering: A Test of Theological Method* (Philadelphia: Westminster Press, 1982) "Self-Giving as the Inner Life of God." Catherine LaCugna's book *God with Us* is helpful in understanding Eastern Trinitarianism. George Hunsinger's 1983 review of Jürgen Moltmann's *Trinity and the Kingdom* in *The Thomist* is very helpful in understanding the superiority of Classical Trinitarianism to some recent efforts.

Preparation and Materials Needed

- Read over carefully the background material and the lesson plan.
- Make decisions where necessary about optional activities, whether to divide into small groups, etc.

- Provide nametags and markers.
- Make enough copies of the worksheets "Baptism" and "The Lord's Supper" (pages 106 and 107) for each class member to have one.
- Cut out cloud shapes from white construction paper or poster paper. Provide one cloud shape for each class member.
- Provide masking tape and a piece of poster paper labeled "Cloud of Witnesses" for the opening activity.
- Invite elders from the mission committee, the Christian Education committee, and the worship committee to visit your class and share information about what the church is doing in these areas. See further instructions for this below under the section "What Does This Mean for Me Today?"
- Hymnals for singing the closing song, "Come Sing, O Church, in Joy."
- A CD or cassette tape player and a recording of "Come Sing, O Church, in Joy." (A recording of this hymn is found on the *Belonging to God* CD and cassette that accompanies the *Belonging to God: A First Catechism* resources) Optional.
- Write the characteristics of a witness (pages 101–102) on newsprint.
- Have newsprint or a wipe board available.

Lesson Plan—Session 7: The Church and the Sacraments. Questions 62—79

WELCOME AND REVIEW

Greet everyone as they come in. Provide nametags if a large group.

Review lessons 1–6 by asking questions 1, 7, 15, 29, 45, and 54 from the catechism and having the class repeat the answers together:

Question 1. What is God's purpose for your life?

God wills that I should live by the grace of the Lord Jesus Christ, for the love of God, and in the communion of the Holy Spirit.

Question 7. What do you believe when you confess your faith in "God the Father Almighty"?

That God is a God of love, and that God's love is powerful beyond measure.

Question 15. What do you believe when you say that God is "Maker of heaven and earth"?

First, that God called heaven and earth, with all that is in them, into being out of nothing simply by the power of God's Word. Second, that by that same power all things are upheld and governed in perfect wisdom, according to God's eternal purpose.

Question 29. What do you believe when you confess your faith in Jesus Christ as "God's only Son"?

That Jesus Christ is a unique person who was sent to do a unique work.

Question 45. Why did Jesus have to suffer as he did?

Because grace is more abundant—and sin more serious—than we suppose. However cruelly we may treat one another, all sin is primarily against God. God condemns sin, yet never judges apart from grace. In giving Jesus Christ to die for us, God took the burden of our sin into God's own self to remove it once and for all. The cross in all its severity reveals an abyss of sin swallowed up by the suffering of divine love.

Question 54. What do you believe when you confess your faith in the Holy Spirit?

Apart from the Holy Spirit, our Lord can neither be loved, nor known, nor served. The Holy Spirit is the personal bond by which Jesus Christ unites us to himself, the teacher who opens our hearts to Christ, and the comforter who leads us to repentance, empowering us to live in Christ's service. As the work of the one Holy Spirit, our love, knowledge, and service of Christ are all inseparably related.

Ask for questions or reflections about material studied in previous sessions.

GETTING STARTED

Constructing a Cloud of Witnesses

One portion of the Apostles' Creed we will be considering today is the "communion of saints," which affirms that "All those who live in union with Christ, whether on earth or with God in heaven, are 'saints.' The ties that bind us in Christ are deeper than any other human relationship." Let's read together Hebrews 12:1–2 (Invite someone to read this passage out loud). Our "cloud of witnesses" includes the entire communion of saints, but there are those that stand out for each of us.

Hand out pieces of white construction paper or poster paper cut into cloud shapes. Invite class members to think of one person in their "cloud of witnesses" who had a significant positive effect on their faith. Ask them to write this person's name on the cloud. After a few minutes, invite them to come forward one at a time and tape their cloud to the wall or a piece of poster board and briefly state who they chose and why. (For example, "My sixth-grade Sunday School teacher, John Smith, because he taught me how to pray." or "My mother, Ann Jones, because she loved me with no strings attached.")

Sing together the first verse of "Blest Be the Tie That Binds" (Hymn #438 in *The Presbyterian Hymnal*).

WHAT DOES THE CHURCH CONFESS?

1. The Church

   Ask participants to jot down some of the words or descriptions that first come to mind when they hear the word "church." Invite those who are willing to share some of their responses and write these on the board or on newsprint.

   Read question 62 responsively.

   Ask, **Where do you see connections between our associations with church and the definition offered by the catechism?**

   What do the creed and the catechism offer as distinguishing characteristics of the church?

   As responses are given, list them on the board. Ask for further explanation for terms such as "holy," "catholic," or "universal." Add your own comments, based on the background material for teachers, where helpful.

2. The Church's Mission

   Read question 63 responsively.

   Ask, **What is the task of a witness? (think of trials, car accidents, marriages)**

   Write responses on the wipe board.

   In his book, *Faith Seeking Understanding*, Daniel Migliore gives the following features of the act of witness: witnesses are sworn to tell the truth; they draw attention not to themselves but to someone or some event distinct from themselves (the event that they attest is singular); and the act of witness is self-involving, requiring personal participation, commitment, and risk.[17]

You may want to write these features of witness on newsprint before class and post it at this time.

Ask, **Drawing off of these features of witnesses and those that we came up with earlier, what are some ways that the church is called to bear witness to God's love for the world in Jesus Christ?**

3. Sacraments

    Read questions 67–70 responsively.

    Look at the question, "What is a sacrament?" (Write this on the board.)

    Ask, **What properties or characteristics of a sacrament are given in the answer to question 68? Look also to question 67 and 69 for more ways of describing what a sacrament is and the functions it performs.**

    List responses on the wipe board (e.g., "instituted by Christ," "visible sign," "means of grace," "seals a promise").

    Ask, **Which of these are more difficult to understand?**

    Invite volunteers to look up Luke 24:30–31, 1 Corinthians 10:16, John 6:51, John 6:56, and 1 Corinthians 11:26. After each verse is read, ask **Which of these points does this verse connect with or help to explain?**

    Work through each point of the definition of sacrament briefly, asking class members to contribute the meaning or providing a brief commentary yourself. (See background information for teachers for assistance in this area.)

4. Baptism and the Lord's Supper

    For this section, divide into groups of three or four. You may either assign half of the groups the work on baptism and half the work on the Lord's Supper, or have each group discuss both sacraments. If each group discusses only one sacrament, have the groups give a brief summary of their findings after you gather back as a large group. Make enough copies of the worksheets "Baptism" and "The Lord's Supper" for each class member to have one (see pages 106–107). Hand these out at this time.

    When the groups have completed their work, bring them back together and share as appropriate.

WHAT DO I THINK?

Choose two of the following topics for further reflection. Remember, it is important to encourage the participants to enter into a dialogue with the catechism, criticizing it when they do not agree and allowing themselves to be questioned by it as well. In short, encourage open and free reflection during this period.

(If your group is larger than twelve, you might consider breaking up into smaller groups of five or six for this portion of the discussion.)

1. Invite the group to share any questions or comments they have about the questions and answers. **Is there a phrase you particularly like? Is there a sentence or concept that is unclear or that you disagree with? If you could choose one phrase to hang on to, what would it be and why?**

2. We confess our belief in the holy catholic church, but our experience shows that the church often does not seem very holy and certainly not unified. **How do we deal with the realities of sin, conflict, and hypocrisy in the church?** Look to catechism questions 61 and 62 for some guidance on this issue.

3. Questions 63–65 address the church's mission: to bear witness to God's love in Jesus Christ.

   How do these answers help us to understand evangelism as something other than church growth?

   How comfortable does our church seem to be with evangelism?

   What makes sharing the gospel difficult for us?

   How can we share the gospel without being pushy or condescending?

   What do you think of the image of "as one beggar tells another where to find bread"? Is this image helpful, challenging, confusing?

   What is at stake in our daily decisions whether or not to bear witness to God's love in word and deed?

4. Some friends who have just had their first child say to you, "Your church has such a pretty sanctuary, and it is right across the street from one of our favorite restaurants. We'd really like to have our child christened there and then have a party afterwards at the restaurant." They are not members of any church and neither has participated in a church since childhood. How would you respond to them? How might you use this occasion to share with them some

of the meaning of baptism and how that guides our understanding of infant baptism?

What Does This Mean for Me Today?

Introduce this section by explaining that you will be hearing about several areas of church life today: mission, Christian education, and worship. Class members will reflect on ways they feel called to join in the life of the congregation.

1. Lead participants in reading questions 63–65 responsively.

    Invite an elder who serves on the mission committee to visit the class and briefly share some of the ways that your congregation is involved in mission. Ask them to mention opportunities for people to join in the mission work of the church.

    Give class members a few minutes to ask questions.

2. Lead participants in reading questions 72, 73, and 79 responsively.

    Invite an elder who serves on the Christian education committee to visit the class and share some of the ways that your congregation seeks to nurture baptized children in the Word of God. Ask them to mention opportunities for class members to participate in nurturing faith in young people.

    Give class members a few minutes to ask questions.

3. Lead participants in reading questions 68 and 78 responsively.

    Invite an elder who serves on the worship committee to visit the class and share how the sacraments are a part of worship in your congregation. Ask them to discuss how baptisms are handled (both infants and adults) and how and when the Lord's Supper is served. If time permits, they could also share other aspects of worship planning and suggest ways that people might become more involved in worship.

    Give class members a few minutes to ask questions.

4. Invite class members to spend a few minutes reflecting on where they may be called to new forms of mission within your church or community. Ask them to write down in their journals any commitments they want to pursue. Encourage them to follow up on this exercise by speaking to one of the elders present about their desire for involvement or asking you whom they should contact if their interest lies in another area.

5. Ask the group, **Where do you see holes in our congregation's mission to the needy? What suggestions do you have for new avenues of mission and ministry?** Write responses on the wipe board or on newsprint.

CLOSING

Sing together "Come Sing, O Church, in Joy!" (Hymn #430 in *The Presbyterian Hymnal*). A sing-a-long recording of this hymn can be found on the *Belonging to God* CD or cassette published by Geneva Press to accompany the resources for *Belonging to God: A First Catechism*.

Close the session with prayer and invite all members to join with you in saying the Lord's Prayer.

Baptism

Share your own memory of baptism, stories that your parents told you about your baptism, or your child's baptism.

Read catechism questions 71–76 together.

Look up Romans 6:3–4, Galatians 3:27, 1 Corinthians 6:11, and Ephesians 4:4–6.

Using the catechism questions and answers and the scripture passages, answer the following questions:

• What are some of the images associated with baptism?

• What is the sign of baptism?

• What are the gifts of baptism?

• What is the central meaning of baptism?

• In what name are we baptized?

• What does the church confess concerning infant baptism?

• What is the role of the congregation in baptism?

The Lord's Supper

Share a memorable experience of the Lord's Supper you have had. It might have been a first communion, on a special retreat, at a wedding, or at a point of crisis in life.

Read catechism questions 77–79 together.

Look up and read Mark 14:22–25, 1 Corinthians 11:23–26, Luke 13:29, and 1 Corinthians 11:28.

Using the catechism questions and answers and the scripture passages, answer the following questions:

- What are the signs of the Lord's Supper?

- Do any of these scripture passages sound like something that you hear in worship when the Lord's Supper is celebrated?

- What happens in the Lord's Supper? List as many things as you can using question 78 and the scripture passages.

- Do you have questions about any of these? If so, bring them back to the large group.

- What does it mean to examine oneself before partaking of the Lord's Supper?

Gifts of God: Forgiveness, Resurrection, and Life Everlasting

The *Study Catechism*: Questions 80–88

Question 80. What do you mean when you speak of "the forgiveness of sins"?

That because of Jesus Christ, God no longer holds my sins against me. Christ alone is my righteousness and my life; Christ is my only hope. Grace alone, not my merits, is the basis on which God has forgiven me in him. Faith alone, not my works, is the means by which I receive Christ into my heart, and with him the forgiveness that makes me whole. Christ alone, grace alone, and faith alone bring the forgiveness I receive through the gospel.

1 Cor. 1:30	1 Tim. 1:1
Rom. 11:6	Eph. 2:8
Rom. 5:15	Rom. 4:16
Rom. 3:28	

Question 81. Does forgiveness mean that God condones sin?

No. God does not cease to be God. Although God is merciful, God does not condone what God forgives. In the death and resurrection of Christ, God judges what God abhors—everything hostile to love—by abolishing it at the very roots. In this judgment the unexpected occurs: good is brought out of evil, hope out of hopelessness, and life out of death. God spares sinners, and turns them from enemies into friends. The uncompromising judgment of God is revealed in the suffering love of the cross.

Hab. 1:13   Isa. 59:15

Heb. 9:22   Rom. 5:8–10

1 Chron. 16:33

Question 82. Does your forgiveness of those who have harmed you depend on their repentance?

No. I am to forgive as I have been forgiven. The gospel is the astonishing good news that while we were yet sinners Christ died for us. Just as God's forgiveness of me is unconditional, and so precedes my confession of sin and repentance, so my forgiveness of those who have harmed me does not depend on their confessing and repenting of their sin. However, when I forgive the person who has done me harm, giving up any resentment or desire to retaliate, I do not condone the harm that was done or excuse the evil of the sin.

Col. 3:13   Mark 11:25

Col. 2:13   Matt. 18:21–22

Heb. 12:14

Question 83. How can you forgive those who have really hurt you?

I cannot love my enemies, I cannot pray for those who persecute me, I cannot even be ready to forgive those who have really hurt me, without the grace that comes from above. I cannot be conformed to the image of God's Son, apart from the power of God's Word and Spirit. Yet I am promised that I can do all things through Christ who strengthens me.

Luke 6:27–28   James 1:17

Rom. 8:29   Phil. 4:13

Question 84. What do you mean when you speak of "the resurrection of the body"?

Because Christ lives, we will live also. The resurrection of the body celebrates our eternal value to God as living persons, each one with a unique and distinctive identity. Indeed, the living Savior who goes before us was once heard, seen, and touched in person, after the discovery of his empty tomb. The resurrection of the body means hope for the whole person, because it is in the

unity of body and soul, not in soul alone, that I belong in life
and in death to my faithful Savior Jesus Christ.

John 14:19	John 11:25
Rom. 6:5	1 Cor. 15:21
1 Cor. 15:42	Col. 1:18

Question 85. What is the nature of resurrection hope?

Resurrection hope is a hope for the transformation of this
world, not a hope for escape from it. It is the hope that evil in all
its forms will be utterly eradicated, that past history will be re-
deemed, and that all the things that ever were will be made
new. It is the hope of a new creation, a new heaven, and a new
earth, in which God is really honored as God, human beings are
truly loving, and peace and justice reign on earth.

Isa. 11:6	Rev. 21:1
Isa. 65:17	2 Pet. 3:13
2 Cor. 5:17	

Question 86. Does resurrection hope mean that we don't have to take action to relieve the suffering of this world?

No. When the great hope is truly alive, small hopes arise
even now for alleviating the sufferings of the present time. Reconciliation—with God, with one another, and with oneself—is
the great hope God has given to the world. While we commit to
God the needs of the whole world in our prayers, we also know
that we are commissioned to be instruments of God's peace.
When hostility, injustice, and suffering are overcome here and
now, we anticipate the end of all things—the life that God
brings out of death, which is the meaning of resurrection hope.

Ps. 27:13	Ps. 33:20–22
Rom. 14:19	Deut. 30:19
Luke 1:78–79	

Question 87. What do you affirm when you speak of "the life everlasting"?

That God does not will to be God without us, but instead
grants to us creatures—fallen and mortal as we are—eternal life.
Communion with Jesus Christ is eternal life itself. In him we

were chosen before the foundation of the world. By him the eternal covenant with Israel was taken up, embodied, and fulfilled. To him we are joined by the Holy Spirit through faith and adopted as children, the sons and daughters of God. Through him we are raised from death to new life. For him we shall live to all eternity.

John 3:16	John 6:54
John 17:3	Rom. 6:22
Rom. 6:23	1 John 2:25
Matt. 25:34	

Question 88. Won't heaven be a boring place?

No. Heaven is our true home, a world of love. There the Spirit shall be poured out into every heart in perfect love. There the Father and the Son are united in the loving bond of the Spirit. There we shall be united with them and one another. There we shall at last see face to face what we now only glimpse as through a distant mirror. Our deepest, truest delights in this life are only a dim foreshadowing of the delights that await us in heaven. "You show me the path of life. In your presence there is fullness of joy; in your right hand are pleasures forevermore" (Ps. 16:11).

John 14:2–3	Matt. 6:20
Matt. 8:11	Col. 1:5
1 Cor. 13:12	

Theological Background

FORGIVENESS OF SINS

All sin is ultimately against God. Therefore, the forgiveness of sins also comes from God, "because of Jesus Christ" (question 80). The precise logic by which Jesus Christ arranges our forgiveness has never been given a single, uniquely authoritative description. This is as it should be, because scripture does not limit us to one such description, and several have served to make the gospel intelligible in different times and places. The one thing all robust understandings of the atonement in Christian theology have in common is that Jesus Christ is understood to stand in our place in some sense.

One prominent view of this logic is that of "penal substitution," in which Christ is understood to suffer the just punishment for our sin, in our place, even though he was innocent. This view is dominated by the idea of justice. The justice of God calls for blood sacrifice to bring peace with God and one another. In the fundamentalist movement of the 1920s there was an effort to make this view uniquely authoritative as one of "the fundamentals," but at least for large segments of the church this movement failed. This failure should not distract us from the fact that penal substitution has been a profoundly meaningful and helpful understanding of Christ's work for many people in many cultures.

Another understanding with great moral and emotional richness is that of Christ as a benefactor who pays our debts. This is a view that has mercy and grace at its heart, in contrast to the legalistic language that goes with the penal substitution view. For C. S. Lewis, during his period of belief in God, but doubt about Christianity, this idea made sense before that of penal substitution did.[18] Jesus himself understood the power of this analogy. In teaching his disciples to pray, he used the idea of indebtedness to represent the sin for which we need God's forgiveness. We still use this analogy in the Presbyterian Church (U.S.A.) when we pray the Lord's Prayer.

P.T. Forsyth explained the doctrine of the atonement in terms of Christ's self-sacrifice. In Forsyth's view, it is not so much that the shedding of Christ's blood as a penal substitution makes possible our peace with God, but that in Christ's execution, God sacrifices Himself for us. It is the element of self-sacrifice, self-giving, not the elements of blood or substitution, that takes first place.

FORGIVENESS IN HUMAN RELATIONSHIPS

In his book, *The Cost of Discipleship*, Dietrich Bonhoeffer coined the term "costly grace" to speak of grace, especially the grace of forgiveness, that is worth having because it is genuine. "Cheap grace," on the other hand, "means forgiveness of sins proclaimed as a general truth, the love of God taught as the Christian 'conception' of God." Cheap grace does not lead to a changed life, "so everything can remain as it was before."[19]

Bonhoeffer's way of putting things is open to misunderstanding because in fact grace is neither cheap nor costly, but free. Yet he makes an important point: Forgiveness is a priceless gift that must be received with awe, wonder, and humility. If we forgive, or expect to be forgiven, as if this were easy, we cheapen it. Though it is free to receive, true forgiveness is hard to seek, and hard to give. Forgiveness is hard to seek because it requires me to say, "I was wrong." I must look at someone I have hurt and take responsibility for what I have done. Forgiveness is costly to seek because it costs me my most treasured possession, my pride.

Our culture offers us easy ways to avoid this pain, but they prove false. The way to reconciliation passes *through* the pain of repentance, not *around* it. By valuing individualism over relationships and self-esteem over virtue, some aspects of our culture invite us to avoid the pain that leads to reconciliation rather than pass through it. Our culture, by its emphasis on individualism, also encourages us to expect forgiveness as a matter of course. But in a world where forgiveness could be taken for granted, human action would have no meaning. Human life would have no moral significance. The passion for life that comes from knowing that tomorrow will be influenced by our actions today would be gone. Life would mean nothing, because it would be going nowhere. In reality, there is no path to forgiveness and peace except the difficult one of acknowledging my wrong, and asking someone else, the person I hurt, to pay the price and suffer the consequences of what I did.

RESURRECTION OF THE BODY AND LIFE EVERLASTING

It is a basic Christian conviction that our identity survives the death of our bodies. With this affirmation, we end this study where we began, with the affirmation that life has purpose. Human life moves toward a definite goal that God has in mind.

We need not be Christians to recognize that if this life is all there is, then utter despair, even the wish never to have been born, is fully justified. Now that we are in a position to look back over the twentieth century, we can see that it has been a horrific blood bath. What has become of the thirty million human beings who were killed in Stalin's purges? Or the ten million or so people Hitler gassed? The fifty thousand Americans killed in Vietnam, to say nothing of those of other nationalities? The number of souls, each a creature of the good God, is mind-numbing. They would be spirit-numbing as well, without our hope for resurrection and life eternal with God.

We fear death, as Karl Barth points out, because life is good. Those who "do not grasp the beauty of this life, cannot grasp the significance of 'resurrection.'" For this word is the answer to death's terror, the terror that this life some day comes to an end, and that this end is the horizon of our existence."[20] Most of us do not want life to end. It is our basic conviction that in fact our lives—truly ourselves—will continue in a different and better form that makes it possible to face death with dignity and poise.

Our hope for resurrection is not simply a hope to be remembered or to have an existence as a pure spirit, but it is quite definitely a hope for a resurrection of the body. It is a hope, not for a continued existence as a disembodied spirit or as some other kind of being, such as an angel, but to live as a perfected human being, in union with God, in a body that is identifiably ours, and yet without all the limitation we now experience.

For Further Study

One classic exposition of the doctrine of the atonement is Gustav Aulen's *Christus Victor*. Aulen's analysis is a bit too neat, in the opinion of many scholars, but it remains a classic, and anyone who wants to know what has been thought about forgiveness needs to check in at Aulen's station.

The classical statement of the penal view of the atonement is St. Anselm of Canterbury's *Cur Deus Homo?* (*St. Anselm: Basic Writings.* trans. S. N. Deane. [La Salle, Ill.: Open Court Publishing Co., 1962], 191–302).

Preparation and Materials Needed

- Read over carefully the background material and the lesson plan.
- Make decisions where necessary about optional activities, whether to divide into small groups, etc.
- Provide nametags and markers.
- Have newsprint or a wipe board available.

Lesson Plan—Session 8: Gifts of God: Forgiveness, Resurrection, and Life Everlasting. Questions 80–88

WELCOME AND REVIEW

Greet everyone as they come in. Provide nametags if a large group.

Review lessons 1–7 by asking questions 1, 7, 15, 29, 45, 54, and 63 from the catechism and having the class repeat the answers together:

> *Question 1. What is God's purpose for your life?*
>
> God wills that I should live by the grace of the Lord Jesus Christ, for the love of God, and in the communion of the Holy Spirit.

Question 7. What do you believe when you confess your faith in "God the Father Almighty"?

That God is a God of love, and that God's love is powerful beyond measure.

Question 15. What do you believe when you say that God is "Maker of heaven and earth"?

First, that God called heaven and earth, with all that is in them, into being out of nothing simply by the power of God's Word. Second, that by that same power all things are upheld and governed in perfect wisdom, according to God's eternal purpose.

Question 29. What do you believe when you confess your faith in Jesus Christ as "God's only Son"?

That Jesus Christ is a unique person who was sent to do a unique work.

Question 45. Why did Jesus have to suffer as he did?

Because grace is more abundant—and sin more serious—than we suppose. However cruelly we may treat one another, all sin is primarily against God. God condemns sin, yet never judges apart from grace. In giving Jesus Christ to die for us, God took the burden of our sin into God's own self to remove it once and for all. The cross in all its severity reveals an abyss of sin swallowed up by the suffering of divine love.

Question 54. What do you believe when you confess your faith in the Holy Spirit?

Apart from the Holy Spirit, our Lord can neither be loved, nor known, nor served. The Holy Spirit is the personal bond by which Jesus Christ unites us to himself, the teacher who opens our hearts to Christ, and the comforter who leads us to repentance, empowering us to live in Christ's service. As the work of the one Holy Spirit, our love, knowledge, and service of Christ are all inseparably related.

Question 63. What is the mission of the church?

The mission of the church is to bear witness to God's love for the world in Jesus Christ.

Ask for questions or reflections about material studied in previous sessions.

GETTING STARTED

Introduce this session by pointing out that one of the focal points of this section of the catechism and the Apostles' Creed is forgiveness. Today we will be exploring how God forgives us, the meaning of forgiveness, and our forgiveness of others. To get us started on this topic, we are going to look at a parable—a teaching story that Jesus told.

Invite class members to turn to Matthew 18:23–35, the parable of the unforgiving servant, and ask a volunteer to read it out loud.

Does anyone have a suggestion for a title for this film?

Imagine that you are Hollywood casting directors, preparing to make a short film version of this parable. **Which stars would you cast in the various roles?** (Lord, slave, slave's wife and children, fellow slaves, etc.)

Ask for volunteers to do a quick run-through of the drama. You will need people to play the parts of a lord, the slave, his fellow slave, and the group of slaves who report to the lord.

WHAT DOES THE CHURCH CONFESS?

1. A Discussion on Forgiveness

   Lead the group in reading catechism questions 80–83 responsively. Direct class members to page 78 in the *Student Guide.*

   Depending on the size and personality of your group, you may choose to divide into small groups for the following discussion. If you do so, write the questions on newsprint or prepare a handout and ask groups to report back on key insights when you bring the groups together.

   Christ alone, grace alone, faith alone — question 80.
   Ask for volunteers to look up and read Ephesians 2:8, Romans 11:6, Romans 5:15, and Romans 3:28.

   Drawing off of the catechism question 80 and these scripture passages, discuss the following questions.
   - What does it mean that we receive forgiveness by Christ alone, grace alone, and faith alone?

- What are we tempted to substitute for Christ alone? For grace alone? For faith alone?
- What are the "works" that we as Christians may fall into relying upon for forgiveness?

Forgive vs. Excuse, Costly vs. Cheap Grace.

Ask for volunteers to look up and read Hebrews 9:22, Romans 5:8–10, and 1 Chronicles 16:33.

Drawing off of catechism question 81 and the scripture passages, discuss the following questions.

- What is the difference between God forgiving our sin and condoning or excusing our sin?
- Is there anything attractive in the notion of God excusing our sin rather than judging and forgiving our sin? (Excusing does not require effort or suffering on God's part, or repentance on our part, no judgment involved)
- Look at 1 Chronicles 16:33. Why would we sing for joy about judgment? Where is there grace and mercy even in the judgment of God? What if God did not judge everything hostile to love? What would be different if God's attitude toward sin and evil were "Whatever"?

Read the following quote from Dietrich Bonhoeffer's *The Cost of Discipleship* on cheap grace and costly grace.

"Cheap grace means grace as a doctrine, a principle, a system. It means forgiveness of sins proclaimed as a general truth, the love of God taught as the Christian 'conception' of God. . . . Cheap grace is the preaching of forgiveness without requiring repentance, baptism without church discipline, Communion without confession, absolution without personal confession. Cheap grace is grace without discipleship, grace without the cross, grace without Jesus Christ, living and incarnate. . . . Costly grace is the treasure hidden in the field; for the sake of it a man will gladly go and sell all that he has. . . . Such grace is costly because it calls us to follow, and it is *grace* because it calls us to follow *Jesus Christ*. It is costly because it costs a man his life, and it is grace because it gives a man the only true life. It is costly because it condemns sin, and grace because it justifies the sinner. Above all, it is *costly* because it cost God the life of his Son: 'ye were bought at a price,' and what has cost God much cannot be cheap for us. Above all, it is grace because God did not reckon his Son too dear a price to pay for our life, but delivered him up for us. Costly grace is the Incarnation of God."[21]

- Where do you see examples of cheap grace or costly grace in the church today, or in your own lives?
- In light of this reading and the catechism questions on forgiveness, reflect on what is at stake in the decision to join the church.

2. A Discussion on the Resurrection of the Body and Life Everlasting
    - Lead the class in reading questions 85–88 responsively.
    - Ask for volunteers to look up and read John 14:19, Romans 6:5, 1 Corinthians 15:42, John 17:3, and Matthew 25:34.
    - Ask the class to list as many movies as they can think of that deal with life after death in some fashion (ghosts, reincarnation, etc.).
    - Ask, **How does the Christian view of resurrection of the body and life everlasting differ from popular portrayals of life after death?**
    - Ask, **What comfort or hope in dealing with death does this doctrine provide?**
    - Invite volunteers to look up and read Isaiah 11:6, 2 Peter 3:13, Psalm 27:13, and Psalm 33:20–22.

    Ask, **What is the nature of Christian hope? Drawing on these scripture passages and the catechism questions and answers, let's list what we hope for (the object of our hope). What basis do we have for our hope? How does our hope influence the way we live?**

    - Heaven—questions 87–88

    Ask for volunteers to look up and read John 14:2–3 and 1 Corinthians 13:12. Direct the group's attention to catechism questions 87 and 88.

    Ask, **What are some of the stereotypical images of heaven?** List these on the wipe board or newsprint.

    Ask, **How do the catechism's description of heaven and that found in the scripture passages differ from these images?**

Ask, **What first thoughts and images come to mind when you hear "true home"? What would make heaven a true home for you?**

Ask, **What does it mean to be fully known and fully loved (1 Corinthians 13:12)? How does this connect with heaven being our true home?**

WHAT DO I THINK?

(If your group is larger than twelve you might consider breaking up into smaller groups of five or six for this portion of the discussion.)

1. Invite the group to share any questions or comments they have about the questions and answers. **Is there a phrase you particularly like? Is there a sentence or concept that is unclear or that you disagree with? If you could choose one phrase to hang on to, what would it be and why?**

2. Forgiving Those Who Hurt Us

   - Look at questions 82 and 83. It sounds good to think of forgiving even our enemies, but what about instances of child abuse, rape, murder, or other heinous crimes? Is it too much for God to demand that we forgive even these crimes? Is there anything in the catechism answers that help us to deal with this issue?

   - Are there ways that the Christian understanding of forgiveness can be misused and misunderstood? Think of situations such as the battered woman who is told she should just forgive her abusive husband and continue living with him.

   - How are we to hold in tension the imperative of forgiveness with the need to fight injustice? Is there anything in the *Catechism*'s definition or explanation of forgiveness that can give us some guidance on this issue?

3. General Hope and Resurrection Hope

   Look at catechism questions 85 and 86. Draw on previous discussions of resurrection hope for this discussion as well.

   - All people engage in hoping and are threatened by hopelessness. How is hope as a human experience connected to Christian hope?

   - What makes Christian hope unique? Is it the basis of our hope or the object of our hope or both?

- How does Christian hope specifically address situations of hopelessness or grief?

- What role does our hope play in our commission to bear witness to God's love in Jesus Christ?

- How is Christian hope passed on to those without hope?

- How can the hope of our community—the church—have an impact on those around us?

What Does This Mean for Me Today?

1. Forgiveness

   Give group members five to ten minutes for silent reflection on the following questions. Invite them to write their responses in their journals.

   Who do I need to forgive?What stands in the way?

   What might I need to ask forgiveness for?

   What holds me back from asking forgiveness?

   Close this time with the following prayer or one of your own.

   "Gracious and loving God, we cannot love our enemies, we cannot pray for those who persecute us, we cannot forgive those who have really hurt us without the grace that comes from you. We cannot be conformed to the image of your son apart from the power of your Word and Spirit. Yet you have promised that we can do all things through Christ who strengthens us. By your grace, grant us the strength to forgive those who hurt us and to seek forgiveness for the wrongs we have done. In Christ's name we pray. Amen."

2. Resurrection Hope

   We have spent some time today speaking of the great hope of the Christian life. Answer 86 states, "When the great hope is truly alive, small hopes arise even now for alleviating the sufferings of the present time."

   Ask, **What are some of your "small hopes" for the present time?** List these on the wipe board or on newsprint.

   Ask, **How might we be instruments of peace in our families, at work, in our neigborhoods, in the church, and in the world?**

Invite participants to choose one of their small hopes and to make a decision to work toward that hope in some way in the week or month ahead. Remind participants that prayer and action go together. Ask participants to write in their journals their small hope and their commitment both to prayer and to action. If you feel that there are members of your group who would like to share what they have chosen, invite volunteers to share.

3. Revisiting the Prologue

Lead the class in reading catechism questions 1–4 responsively.

Ask, **Have you gained any new insights on grace, love, and communion in this course?**

Invite group members to flip through their journals and the catechism questions. Ask, **Have you come to any new understandings of God's purpose for your life that you want to hang on to after this class is over? Do you have any new images for who you are called to be (for example, "an instrument of peace" [answer 86], "a mirror which reflects God's love" [answer 18], "patient in adversity, thankful in blessing, and courageous against injustice" [answer 23]?**

CLOSING

Draw the group's attention to the closing exercise in the *Student Guide*, "Where Will You Go From Here?" and encourage them to take the time at home for this final reflection.

Lead the group in saying together the Apostles' Creed.

Close by singing the Doxology together as a prayer.

Notes

1. Karl Barth, *Dogmatics in Outline* (New York: HarperCollins Publishers, Inc., 1959): 15–16.
2. Arthur C. McGill, *Suffering: A Test of Theological Method* (Philadelphia: The Westminster Press, 1968), 60.
3. The phrase is John Leith's, from *The Reformed Imperative: What the Church Has to Say that No One Else Can Say* (Louisville, Ky.: Westminster/John Knox Press, 1988).
4. Robert Sokolowski, *The God of Faith and Reason* (Washington, D.C.: Catholic University of American Press, 1995).
5. John H. Leith, *Crisis in the Church: the Plight of Theological Education* (Louisville, Ky.: Westminster/John Knox Press, 1997), 29.
6. Diogenes Allen, *Christian Belief in a Post-modern World* (Louisville, Ky.: Westminster/John Knox Press, 1989).
7. Marilynne Robinson, *The Death of Adam: Essays on Modern Thought* (Boston: Houghton Mifflin, 1999), 71.
8. Karl Barth, *Credo*, trans. J. S. McNab (London: Hodder & Stoughton, 1936), 48–50.
9. Dallas Willard, "How To Be a Disciple." *Christian Century* (April 22–29, 1998), 431.
10. Barth, *Credo*, 60.
11. Dorothy L. Sayers, "The Execution of God." *Radio Times*, March 23, 1945.
12. Barth, *Credo*, 85.
13. John Calvin, *Institutes of the Christian Religion*, ed. John T. McNeil, trans. Ford Lewis Battles (Philadelphia: Westminster Press, 1960), 2.16.15.
14. Calvin, *Institutes*, op. cit. 1.9.3.
15. Karl Barth, *Church Dogmatics* 1/2. (Edinburgh: T. & T. Clark, 1975), 55.
16. Augustine, chapter 26, *On Catechizing the Uninstructed*. See also John Calvin, *Institutes*, op. cit. 4.14.1.
17. Daniel L. Migliore, *Faith Seeking Understanding* (Grand Rapids: Wm. B. Eerdmans Publishing Company, 1991), 207.
18. C. S. Lewis, *Mere Christianity* (New York: Macmillan Publishing Co., 1952), 44.
19. Dietrich Bonhoeffer, *The Cost of Discipleship* (Magnolia, Mass.: Peter Smith Publishers, Inc., 1983).
20. Karl Barth, *Dogmatics in Outline*, trans. G. T. Thomson (London: SCM Press, 1949), 153.
21. Bonhoeffer, *Cost of Discipleship*.